UNDERSTANDING TRAUMA AND PTSD IN LIGHT OF ISLAMIC AND MODERN PSYCHOLOGY

A Self-Help Guide with Workbook Elements to Heal

Immad Uddin Khan

Cover design by: Immad Uddin Khan

Dedication
To every survivor finding the courage to heal.

Acknowledgments
I'm grateful to colleagues for their insights. Special thanks to scholars who shared Islamic psychology wisdom. And to every community that taught me resilience.

CONTENTS

From Trauma to Transformation – Hope and Growth Beyond PTSD

Preface: A Journey Towards Healing

For the past four years, I have had the privilege of working with individuals looking to overcome trauma.Witnessing their struggles and their eventual emergence towards healing has been a deeply moving experience.

In my practice, I observed a crucial gap. While clinical science offered invaluable insights and methodologies, its objective nature sometimes lacked the warmth and empathetic approach needed to truly resonate with the human experience of trauma.

Conversely, while spiritual wisdom provides comfort and meaning, its abstract nature at times feels disconnected from the immediate and tangible realities of trauma's impact.

This guide represents my attempt to bridge this divide.

It is born from a conviction that true healing requires in-depth understanding offered by clinical science and the profound wisdom and solace found in spiritual traditions.

Within these pages, you will discover clear and accessible explanations of trauma and its effects, alongside practical, evidence-based exercises designed to facilitate healing and growth. Recognizing the diverse needs and beliefs of those on this journey, I have also incorporated faith-based reflections and callouts, offering a spiritual dimension to the healing process.

I encourage you to approach this guide with patience and self-compassion. Work through the material at a pace that feels comfortable and sustainable for you. Experiment with the various tools and techniques presented, and embrace those that resonate most deeply with your individual needs and circumstances.

Please know, with unwavering certainty, that you are not alone in this journey.

Healing from trauma is a courageous and transformative process, and I hope this guide serves as a supportive companion along your path towards wholeness and well-being.

◆ ◆ ◆

INTRODUCTION

Trauma is a fact of life for many people – but it is also something we can heal from. In simple terms, trauma refers to intensely disturbing experiences that overwhelm our ability to cope and have lasting negative effects on our well-being. These events might include violence, abuse, serious accidents, disasters, or any situation where we feel terrified, helpless, or in danger.

Such experiences can leave deep emotional wounds. In the immediate aftermath, it's normal to feel upset, on edge, or in shock – our brains and bodies are processing what happened. Most people will recover in time as these reactions fade. However, some find that their symptoms don't improve and even worsen over time, disrupting daily life.

This may indicate post-traumatic stress disorder, or PTSD.

PTSD is a mental health condition that can develop after trauma when our natural recovery processes get ***"stuck."***

People with PTSD often feel as if they are reliving the trauma or cannot escape its shadow. They may have nightmares, flashbacks, constant anxiety, or feel numb and detached.

It's as if part of the brain is still in emergency mode, even when no current danger exists. PTSD is more common than many realize – by some estimates, around 70% of people worldwide experience at least one traumatic event in their lifetime (WHO), and while most do not develop PTSD, a significant minority do.

In the general population, a few percent will have PTSD at some point (about 6–8% in a U.S. context, for example). In any case, trauma and PTSD affect people of all ages and backgrounds.

This book is for everyone – teens, adults, survivors, supporters, and even trainee therapists – to understand what trauma is, how it impacts us, and how we can recover and grow from it.

What you can expect

Before you step onto the healing process, you need to know what's happening in the brain, body, and mind. You'll learn the signs and symptoms of trauma to recognize in yourself or others. Once we are clear about the definitions, we will then delve into approaches to healing.

We'll break down evidence-based therapeutic frameworks – like trauma-focused cognitive-behavioral therapy (TF-CBT), EMDR, Acceptance and Commitment Therapy (ACT), and somatic therapies – in accessible terms, so you know what tools are out there. We'll also discuss what it means for a caregiver or organization to be trauma-informed, ensuring that anyone supporting survivors does so with safety and compassion in mind.

Throughout the book, you'll find **practical strategies** and **coping tools** you can try right away – from grounding exercises to journaling prompts and relaxation techniques. These are like a first aid kit for emotional distress, to help you regain calm in the moment. You'll also find guided **exercises and reflections** to gently work through your experiences at your own pace. Think of these as workbook sections embedded in the chapters – chances to pause and apply what you're learning to yourself.

Coming from a South Asian background, I acknowledge that healing is not "*one size fits all.*"

Cultural background, family upbringing, and personal beliefs influence how we experience and heal from trauma. For that reason, the book includes optional callout sections on **faith-based insights** – particularly from an Islamic psychology perspective – where relevant.

Trauma can raise spiritual questions like "Why did this happen to me?" or "How can I find meaning after this?" Different faith traditions offer their own answers.

Readers interested in spiritual framing, especially Muslim readers, may find comfort and guidance in these insights. If that's not for you, you can skip those sections without losing the main thread.

Above all, this book is meant to be **clear, supportive, and empowering**. The tone is conversational, as if we're talking through these topics together, and I have tried to avoid jargon or technical language whenever possible. When I do introduce an important clinical term, I'll explain it in plain language. You do not need any background in psychology to benefit from this book.

Whether you're a survivor of trauma, someone supporting a loved one, a student learning about therapy, or just a curious reader, our goal is that you come away with a deeper understanding of how trauma affects people and a toolbox of strategies to foster healing and growth.

A quick note before we dive in: **Healing from trauma is absolutely possible.**

It's not easy and it's not fast – it's a journey that may zigzag with ups and downs. There is no magic cure and no simple forgetting. But with the right support, the wounds of trauma can mend. Many people not only recover but also experience positive changes in the aftermath, discovering new strengths, purpose, and resilience (often called post-traumatic growth).

As we explore the challenges trauma brings, we will also keep sight of hope. You are not "broken" beyond repair – you are **injured**, and injuries can heal.

As you read, please be gentle with yourself.

If at any point you feel overwhelmed or triggered by the material (for instance, if it reminds you of painful memories), feel free to take a break. Use the coping skills discussed to relax yourself - practice a few deep breaths, ground yourself in the present, or reach out to someone you trust.

Your well-being comes first.

When you're ready, return to the book. It will wait for you.

With that in mind, let's begin our journey by understanding what trauma really is and how it affects the brain, body, and behavior. Knowledge is power – by learning about trauma and PTSD, you're already taking the first step toward healing.

CHAPTER 1: UNDERSTANDING TRAUMA

Trauma isn't just the bad event itself – it's how that event impacts you. Psychologists note that two people could live through the same disaster; one may carry it as trauma, while the other, though shaken, might not experience long-term effects.

Trauma is highly personal. In general, we call something traumatic when it's so distressing that it leaves you feeling powerless, intensely afraid, or overwhelmed, and these feelings persist.

The American Psychological Association defines trauma as

> *"Any disturbing experience that results in significant fear, helplessness, dissociation, confusion, or other disruptive feelings intense enough to have a long-lasting negative effect on a person's attitudes, behavior, and other aspects of functioning."*

In simpler terms, trauma is a psychological injury. Just as a physical injury like a burn might leave a scar, an emotional injury from trauma can leave an invisible "scar" that alters how we feel and act.

Traumatic experiences can take many forms. Some are **acute** single events – for example, a car accident, a natural disaster, or a one-time assault. Others are **chronic or repeated** trauma – such as ongoing childhood abuse, neglect, domestic violence, or living in a war zone. There are also **collective traumas**, which affect a large group or community (for instance, a terrorist attack or a pandemic).

We sometimes differentiate “Big T” traumas (life-threatening events, severe abuse, etc.) from “small t” traumas (less obvious events that still overwhelm you – perhaps bullying or the sudden loss of a job). All can be traumatic; it depends on the person’s experience. It’s important to remember that trauma is defined by its impact **on you**, not by some objective checklist of how “bad” the event was. If it felt devastating and has caused lingering distress, then it was traumatic for you, regardless of how it might look to someone else.

How common is trauma?

Unfortunately, trauma is very common. By adulthood, most people have been through at least one event that could be considered traumatic. A large international survey across 24 countries found that over **70%** of respondents had experienced a traumatic event in their lifetime. (In that study, common traumas included sudden loss of a loved one, witnessing death or serious injury, accidents, physical or sexual violence, etc.) Many had experienced multiple traumas; about 30% had been through **four or more** separate traumatic events.

In the U.S., other surveys have found around 60% of men and 50% of women experience at least one trauma in life. So if you have gone through something traumatic, you are far from alone. Trauma touches people of all ages, cultures, and walks of life – it “has no boundaries” as one report noted.

However, not everyone who goes through trauma will suffer long-term. In fact, most people show resilience: they may be very distressed at first (which is normal), but over weeks and months they gradually recover.

So when does trauma lead to lasting problems, and why?

A key factor is whether that inner “scar” forms. In the immediate aftermath of a horrific event, **fear, anxiety, sadness, anger, shock, or grief** are common reactions. You might have nightmares, feel jumpy, or avoid thinking about what happened – initially.

These reactions are the mind’s way of processing an abnormal situation. For most, they fade within a few weeks. The mind and body naturally seek a return to balance. People often talk with loved ones, draw on coping skills, and overtime start to feel like themselves again. In technical terms, this is sometimes called an acute stress reaction, and it usually resolves.

However, if the experience was especially overwhelming, or if you lack support, or have a history of previous trauma, the stress might not resolve so easily.

Instead, those reactions can persist and even intensify, developing into post-traumatic stress disorder (PTSD). In PTSD, it's as if the brain gets stuck in danger mode and cannot move on.

Before we get into PTSD in depth, it's worth dispelling a myth:

Trauma is not a sign of weakness.

If you're struggling after a horrible event, it's not because you're *"not strong enough*" or "*should have handled it better.*" Trauma reactions – even very severe ones – are **your mind and body's normal responses** to extremely abnormal events.

In fact, what we call PTSD is in some ways a **protective** mechanism that has gone into overdrive.

Later on in the book, we'll discuss exactly how PTSD works, but for now, just understand that anyone can be traumatized if the circumstances are extreme enough. It has nothing to do with courage or character.

For example, even battle-hardened soldiers can develop PTSD – not because they lack bravery, but because humans aren't made to endure endless life-threatening stress. Similarly, a usually resilient person might be floored by a one-time incident if it catches them at a vulnerable moment. Everyone has a breaking point.

It's also important to note that **trauma can be invisible to others**.

People might carry profound pain from childhood abuse or from experiences like miscarriage, racial discrimination, or medical emergencies, and those around them might have no idea.

Just because someone isn't a combat veteran or didn't survive a headline-making disaster doesn't mean they haven't suffered trauma. We should be careful not to invalidate someone's trauma by saying "It wasn't that bad" or "Others have had it worse."

Each person's nervous system responds in its own way. If it mattered to them, it matters. Period.

In the next chapter, we'll look at PTSD – the condition that sometimes results from trauma. Understanding PTSD will give us a framework for the common patterns of symptoms that many trauma survivors experience.

First, here's a quick recap of key points about trauma:

- **Trauma is an injury**, not a weakness – a traumatic event overwhelms one's ability to cope and can have lasting emotional effects.
- **Traumas can be big or small, one-time or ongoing.** What matters is the impact on the person, not just the external facts of the event.
- **Trauma is extremely common.** Most people experience at least one traumatic event in life, though not all develop long-term problems.
- **Initial reactions** (shock, fear, anxiety, etc.) are normal and usually fade with time for many people.
- **Risk factors** for lasting trauma effects include the severity and duration of the event, prior trauma history, lack of support, and

individual differences. Trauma can happen to anyone, but not everyone will respond the same way.

- **You are not alone, and you are not to blame** for the harm you suffered. The responsibility lies with the event or perpetrator, not the survivor.

With that foundation, let’s move on to understand PTSD more deeply – essentially, what happens when trauma’s aftermath does not fade away, and instead becomes a persistent disorder.

CHAPTER 2: UNDERSTANDING PTSD

We've established that it's normal to have some stress after trauma. **Post-Traumatic Stress Disorder (PTSD)** is diagnosed when those stress reactions don't resolve and begin to cause significant disruption in a person's life. In PTSD, the trauma isn't just a memory – it feels like it's still happening or about to happen again, over and over.

The formal criteria for PTSD (according to mental health professionals) require that symptoms last at least ***one month*** after the traumatic event and are severe enough to interfere with daily functioning. In other words, we all might be extremely upset for a couple of weeks after a trauma – but if you're still experiencing intense symptoms beyond a month, and especially if things are getting worse or affecting your work, school, or relationships, it could be PTSD and it's time to seek help.

What do PTSD symptoms actually look like? Doctors and psychologists group them into **four main categories**:

1. **Intrusive memories (Re-experiencing):** This means unwanted thoughts or even vivid flashbacks of the trauma that intrude into your mind. You might have **nightmares** about what happened, or even flashbacks where you momentarily feel like you're right back in it, reliving the event. Certain "triggers" – like a loud sound, a particular smell, or a place – can set off intense distress, as if the trauma is happening again. Even if you're trying not to think about it, these memories and feelings pop up involuntarily and cause a lot of anguish. Physical reactions can

accompany this; for example, your heart races or you break into a sweat when reminded of the trauma.

2. **Avoidance:** Because those trauma memories and reminders are so upsetting, people with PTSD often go to great lengths to **avoid** anything associated with the trauma. This can mean avoiding external things – like refusing to drive after a bad car accident, staying away from the neighborhood where something bad happened, or avoiding news stories that are reminders. It also includes avoiding internal reminders – trying not to talk about it, not think about it, perhaps using alcohol or substances to numb out thoughts. Avoidance is understandable (no one wants to feel pain), but it can become very limiting because it shrinks the person's world and prevents them from processing the trauma.

3. **Negative changes in thinking and mood:** Trauma can fundamentally alter your thoughts and feelings about yourself and the world. People with PTSD often develop persistent negative beliefs – for instance, "I'm broken," "I can't trust anyone," or "The world is completely dangerous." You might feel **guilt or shame**, even blaming yourself for what happened (survivors of abuse often carry irrational shame). Chronic **fear, anger, or horror** are common emotional states. Some feel detached or numb – unable to experience happiness or love. You might lose interest in activities you used to enjoy, or feel isolated from others. In short, your emotional landscape turns bleak. Loved ones might notice you've "changed" – for example, a once-outgoing person may become emotionally withdrawn after trauma.

4. **Changes in physical and emotional reactions (Hyperarousal):** This set of symptoms is like your body's "alarm system" is stuck in the on position. You may feel **constantly on guard** or jittery, as if danger could strike at any moment. This is called hypervigilance. It comes with an

exaggerated **startle response** – e.g. you jump dramatically at sudden noises or movements. Sleep problems are very common; it can be hard to fall asleep or stay asleep (the body doesn't want to let its guard down). Concentration can be difficult because part of you is always scanning the environment for threats. Irritability and angry outbursts can happen, sometimes seemingly out of nowhere – your "fight or flight" system is hair-trigger, so you may overreact to minor provocations. Some people engage in reckless or self-destructive behavior (like driving too fast or drinking heavily) – this can be an attempt to either feel something different or because normal risk assessment is altered.

These are the core symptoms of PTSD. To summarize in plainer language: people with PTSD often relive the trauma mentally (even when they don't want to), try hard to avoid anything that reminds them of it, experience pervasive negative feelings and beliefs as a result of the trauma, and feel physically keyed up all the time.

It's a heavy burden to carry. No wonder that PTSD can affect one's ability to function day-to-day – it can strain relationships, make it hard to hold a job or concentrate in school, and severely lower quality of life.

It's worth noting that **PTSD symptoms may not appear immediately** in some cases. While many people develop symptoms within days or weeks after the event, others might not notice a big problem until months or even years later.

For example, someone might seem to cope fine with a trauma at first, but six months down the line something triggers them and then the PTSD pattern emerges. Delayed-onset PTSD is recognized – sometimes the psyche basically keeps things together until some stressor or change (like returning home from deployment) causes the symptoms to surface.

Also, PTSD can look a bit different in **children**. Young children might not have the vocabulary to describe their inner experience. Instead, they may express trauma through play (for instance, repeatedly acting out aspects of the trauma with toys) or through generalized fears and separation anxiety.

They might have nightmares that aren't obviously related to the trauma. Children can also regress (e.g. a potty-trained child starts bedwetting again, or they become extra clingy). Teens with PTSD often show similar signs to adults, but sometimes more behavioral acting-out (impulsivity, aggression) or aches and pains. Chapter 6 will discuss recognizing trauma signs in different ages and contexts in more detail.

It's very common for PTSD to **occur alongside other issues**. Depression, anxiety disorders, and substance use problems frequently co-occur with PTSD. For example, someone with PTSD might start drinking heavily to sleep or forget, and end up with an alcohol problem. Or they might develop depression due to the hopelessness and withdrawal PTSD can cause.

Sometimes the symptoms overlap – trouble sleeping and concentrating could be from PTSD, depression, or both. What this means for those suffering is that trauma can have a big ripple effect. It's not just flashbacks or anxiety; it can touch many aspects of mental health.

The good news is that treating PTSD often improves those other areas too.

Why do some get PTSD and others don't?

This is a complex question and research is ongoing. We know certain factors increase risk: experiencing multiple traumas over time (cumulative impact), trauma that occurs in childhood, interpersonal traumas like rape (which tend to be more shattering), having little support after the event, or having existing mental health vulnerabilities can all raise the likelihood of PTSD.

Biological factors (like genes, or differences in how one's brain responds to stress hormones) also play a role. Interestingly, if someone has had adversity in childhood, it can prime their system to be more susceptible to PTSD after a trauma later in life. That doesn't mean it's inevitable – just more likely. Conversely, factors like strong social support, coping skills, and certain personality traits (like optimism or resilience) might buffer against PTSD.

It's critical to understand that **PTSD is not a sign of personal failure**. If you develop PTSD, you did not "do something wrong." As mentioned, anyone can develop it given severe enough trauma and circumstances. It's a brain and body response.

In fact, it's often said that PTSD is a normal response to abnormal events. Think of it this way: if you suffer a bad fall, you might break a bone; if you suffer a bad trauma, you might "break" your sense of safety. PTSD is the injury that results. Just like we'd treat the broken bone, PTSD can be treated and healed too.

When to seek help

If you or someone you care about has been through a trauma and is still experiencing significant distress after a month or more, especially if it's getting worse or interfering with life, it's important to reach out for help.

PTSD is not something one should just "tough out" alone. Often, professional therapy is needed to recover. Reaching out might mean talking to a doctor, a counselor, or a psychologist/therapist who specializes in trauma. There are very effective treatments available now, which we'll explore in upcoming chapters. The sooner you get support, generally the better – early intervention can prevent symptoms from entrenching. If there are suicidal thoughts or feelings of harming yourself because the pain is so great, seek help immediately (such as calling a crisis line or emergency services).

Suicidal feelings can accompany PTSD, especially if someone feels hopeless or blames themselves deeply. We want you to stay safe and know that there is hope, even if it's hard to see in the dark moments.

Before moving on, let's quickly recap PTSD in a nutshell:

- **PTSD** is a condition where the effects of trauma don't fade and instead persist, causing significant life problems. It involves re-experiencing the trauma, avoidance, negative mood/thought changes, and hyperarousal.

- It’s only diagnosed if symptoms last >1 month post-trauma and cause real impairment. (Symptoms right after trauma are normal; they become PTSD if they stick and worsen.)
- People with PTSD aren’t “staying in the past” on purpose – their brains are stuck in survival mode. It’s like a smoke alarm that keeps blaring even without fire.
- PTSD often comes with guilt, shame, or feeling “crazy,” but remember it’s a known medical condition and a treatable one.
- Not everyone develops PTSD after trauma; various risk factors exist, but sometimes it occurs without a clear reason. Avoid judgment.
- If you suspect PTSD in yourself or someone else, encourage seeking professional help. Effective therapies exist, and earlier is better.

Now that we have an understanding of PTSD’s definition and symptoms, the next step is to learn why these symptoms happen. What is going on in the brain and body that causes flashbacks, anxiety, and all these reactions?

By learning the science of trauma’s impact, we can start to demystify it. It’s not “just in your head” in the dismissive sense – it’s in your brain wiring, your nervous system, your whole being.

The good news is, what is wired in by trauma can be rewired with healing. Let’s explore the biology of trauma next.

CHAPTER 3: HOW TRAUMA AFFECTS THE BRAIN

Trauma doesn't only leave psychological memories; it can actually **change the structure and function of your brain**. This is a fascinating and important area of research. Understanding it can help explain why you might feel and behave differently after a traumatic experience. It also shows that PTSD is physiological, not imagined – your brain is literally in a different state. In this chapter, we'll break down the brain changes in simple terms, and then see how these changes produce the symptoms we just discussed.

Think of the brain as having a few key players in trauma and stress responses:

- The **amygdala** – often called the brain's "fear center". It's an almond-shaped cluster deep in the brain that constantly scans for threats and triggers the alarm response (fight/flight) when it perceives danger.

- The **prefrontal cortex (PFC)** – the front part of the brain (behind your forehead) responsible for reasoning, impulse control, and regulation of emotions. It's like the brain's wise CEO that can calm down the amygdala and say "It's okay, we're actually safe now."
- The **hippocampus** – a seahorse-shaped structure crucial for memory, especially for putting memories in context and distinguishing past from present.
- Other areas like the **cerebellum** (involved in coordination and emotional regulation) and the brain's reward system (which involves

dopamine) also play roles, but we'll focus on the big three above for simplicity.

In a **normal stress situation**, these parts work together: The amygdala senses danger and shouts "Emergency!"; the body floods with stress hormones (like adrenaline and cortisol) to prepare you to fight or run; meanwhile, if the threat passes, your prefrontal cortex steps in to calm things down ("False alarm, stand down") and your hippocampus files the event away as a memory of something that happened in the past. You might be shaken, but you know it's over.

In **traumatic stress**, that system gets massively overloaded. The amygdala's alarm is screaming. The prefrontal cortex (which would normally soothe things) can get overwhelmed and kind of go offline – so the "brakes" on the amygdala fail. The hippocampus, under high stress, doesn't encode memories in a neat, orderly way; it may store fragments of memory without a clear timestamp. This is why trauma memories can be so disorganized and flashback-like – your brain stored them in a state-specific, sensory way (sights, sounds, sensations) rather than as a coherent narrative in the past tense.

Over time, repeated trauma or severe trauma can lead to **measurable changes** in these brain regions. Studies using brain scans have found, for example, that people with PTSD often have an overactive amygdala and an underactive prefrontal cortex, especially a part of the PFC called the **ventromedial PFC** (which is key to regulating emotional responses).

In essence, the brain's fear alarm is turned up high, and the part that should quiet that alarm is turned down. This explains why folks with PTSD might feel fear or panic in situations where others feel fine – their fear circuitry is on a hair-trigger.

Additionally, the **hippocampus** in many PTSD sufferers shows abnormalities. Research has noted reductions in volume of the hippocampus in some people with PTSD, suggesting that chronic stress hormones can actually shrink it or at least impair its functioning. One study found that more severe PTSD was linked to physical indentations (signs of volume loss or changes) in the right amygdala and right hippocampus.

The hippocampus helps distinguish between past and present; if it's not functioning well, you can see why a memory might feel like it's happening now (the brain loses the context that "this was then, not now"). It also contributes to memory problems – like not being able to recall parts of the trauma or, conversely, being unable to stop recalling it.

There are other brain changes too. Some studies show **reduced gray matter** in parts of the prefrontal cortex (gray matter is the working tissue of the brain). Changes have been noted in the **cerebellum** as well (which might relate to coordination of emotional responses).

The brain's **reward system** can also be blunted in PTSD – meaning things that should feel good or positive don't register as strongly, possibly contributing to numbness or depression. On the flip side, in certain cases of PTSD where people dissociate (detach emotionally) during trauma, there's evidence of reduced amygdala activity and increased frontal activity – essentially a different subtype where the brain copes by shutting down feelings (we won't dig too deep into that, but it shows PTSD isn't one-size-fits-all in the brain).

To simplify: **Trauma can rewire the brain to be stuck in survival mode.** The amygdala becomes like an oversensitive smoke detector – it goes off at the slightest hint of smoke (any reminder of trauma). The prefrontal cortex, which should talk down the amygdala, struggles to do so, as if its power is weakened. And the hippocampus is having trouble laying down proper memory files, so traumatic memories keep intruding as raw sensory fragments and emotional states, not as processed, time-stamped stories. These brain changes directly translate to PTSD symptoms:

- An overactive amygdala and weakened frontal control leads to **exaggerated fear responses**, constant sense of threat, anxiety, and startle reactions. It also makes it hard to regulate emotions – the fear/anger can flood without the usual regulation.
- A dysfunctional hippocampus leads to **intrusive memories and flashbacks**, as well as difficulty telling the past from present (so a firework = panic attack because it triggers the same fear as a gunshot in war, for example). It also contributes to memory blanks or fragmentation regarding the trauma.

- Changes in reward circuitry explain why people might feel **numb or joyless** – activities that used to be rewarding don't register the same, leading to low motivation or even turning to risky behaviors to feel something (like substance use).
- Overall brain hyperarousal means **difficulty relaxing or sleeping** – the whole system is on edge, as if the brain says "Never again will I be caught off guard," so it's hypervigilant 24/7.

It's truly remarkable (and sad) how efficient the brain is at adapting to trauma for survival, and how those adaptations cause so much distress in normal life. The brain is doing what it thinks it must to protect you – staying alert, remembering the danger, avoiding anything similar.

But in PTSD, these protections overshoot, becoming maladaptive.

It's like an autoimmune disease of the psyche: the defense (fear response) ends up attacking the self by never shutting off.

On a biochemical level, trauma can alter stress hormone systems. People with PTSD often have an exaggerated release of adrenaline and related stress chemicals even to minor triggers. The **nervous system** (specifically the sympathetic nervous system, which controls fight-or-flight) becomes easily activated, while the **parasympathetic** (rest-and-digest) has trouble kicking in.

This can lead to chronic elevations in heart rate and blood pressure under stress, and contributes to why trauma is linked with health issues (which we'll discuss in the next chapter on the body). Some research even suggests inflammation markers are higher in those with PTSD – the body's in a state of red alert.

It's not all bad news, though. One of the most important discoveries is that **the brain can heal and rewire**. This ability is called **neuroplasticity**. Our brains are not fixed; they change with experience and training throughout life. Just as trauma caused these brain changes, recovery can cause healing changes.

For example, brain scans have shown that effective therapy can **restore more normal patterns** of brain activity. In one study, after a course of cognitive behavioral therapy (CBT) for anxiety (a similar mechanism to PTSD), patients' overactive amygdalae settled down to more normal activity levels.

In another study of people with PTSD undergoing EMDR (a therapy we'll explain later), they found excessive prefrontal activity decreased to normal levels – meaning the brain wasn't working so hard to suppress trauma once healing occurred. These are small studies, but they offer hope that treatment doesn't just change how you feel, it can literally change your brain.

Even practices like mindfulness meditation have been shown to strengthen the calming parts of the nervous system.

To summarize this chapter in non-technical terms: **Trauma is like a rewiring of your brain's alarm system**. It makes the alarm super sensitive and the off-switch weak.

This explains a lot of PTSD symptoms – your brain and body are acting as if danger is still around every corner. But with proper treatment and coping, you can retrain your brain. It can learn, for instance, that a particular trigger (like a crowded mall or a certain cologne scent) is not actually dangerous, even though it's similar to something from the trauma. Over time, the alarm response can diminish. The brain's natural healing can resume once we give it the right conditions (safety, therapy, time).

We'll see in later chapters how therapies like **TF-CBT and EMDR** are essentially techniques to help the brain reprocess and file away the trauma safely – in a sense, they help the frontal cortex and hippocampus regain control over the runaway amygdala. For now, the key takeaway is: **PTSD is brain-based**. Knowing this can replace self-blame with understanding. If you've been thinking "Why can't I just get over it? What's wrong with me?" – realize that your brain is doing this, not because you're weak, but because it was trying to protect you and got stuck in overprotection mode. And brains can change.

EXERCISE: GROUNDING YOURSELF WITH 5-4-3-2-1

After learning about how trauma affects the brain, you might find that even reading about these things brings up some anxious feelings or reminders of your own experiences. Let's pause and practice a simple **grounding exercise**. Grounding means bringing your attention to the present and to your senses, which can help calm the amygdala when it's firing off.

This is called the **5-4-3-2-1 technique** for grounding in the here-and-now:

1. **5 – Sight:** Look around you and name **five** things you can see right now. It could be "the pattern of the carpet, the blue sky out the window, a coffee mug on the table, a wall clock, my own hands."

2. **4 – Touch:** Now focus on **four** things you can feel through touch. For example, "my feet pressing on the floor, the cool air on my skin, the fabric of my shirt on my shoulders, the smooth surface of the table under my hand."

3. **3 – Sound:** Next, listen for **three** things you can hear. It might be "the hum of the air conditioner, birds chirping outside, the sound of my breathing."

4. **2 – Smell:** Identify **two** things you can smell. If you're in a place with no obvious smells, you can think of your two favorite scents instead (like coffee and fresh grass). Or take a quick walk to find some scents ("I smell soap on my hands, and the leather of my chair").

5. **1 – Taste:** Finally, notice **one** thing you can taste. Maybe it's just the aftertaste of something you ate, or even just "I taste the mint of my toothpaste" or plain water. If you don't notice a taste, you can take a sip of water or imagine the taste of a favorite food.

As you go through these five senses, take your time. Breathe slowly. This exercise works by redirecting your brain away from distressing thoughts and into the present moment, grounding you in your body and environment. It's surprisingly effective for reducing acute anxiety or dissociation.

By the time you finish 5-4-3-2-1, you should feel more centered and in control. If not, you can repeat the cycle or modify it (sometimes I do another round with different items, or focus especially on touch and sight). This is a tool you can use anytime you feel triggered or panicky – it's simple and always available (your senses are with you everywhere!).

Reflect: How did you feel before and after doing 5-4-3-2-1?

Could you notice a shift, even a small one, in your level of calmness or how "present" you felt? Everyone's experience is a bit different, but many people report that their racing heart slows down and their mind feels less caught up in the trauma after doing this.

Remember this technique; we'll refer back to grounding later as we discuss coping strategies.

Now that we've covered the brain's role in trauma, the next chapter will look at how trauma affects the **rest of the body** and our physical health. The mind and body are deeply connected. Trauma is not just "in your head" – it can have real, tangible effects on your body as well. Understanding those will give us a full picture of the impact of trauma.

♦ ♦ ♦

CHAPTER 4: HOW TRAUMA AFFECTS THE BODY

When we say someone "went through a trauma," we often focus on the emotional and psychological toll. But make no mistake: **the body keeps score** of trauma as well (to borrow the phrase from Dr. Bessel van der Kolk).

Our physical body responds to traumatic stress in numerous ways, both immediate and long-term.

Have you ever felt your heart pounding with fear, or your stomach twisting with anxiety?

That's the body's side of the trauma response. In this chapter, we'll explore the physiological aspect: from the fight-or-flight response, to the chronic health effects that trauma survivors might experience.

Fight, Flight, or Freeze: When faced with a sudden threat, our bodies automatically prepare to either fight the danger or run away (flight). This is the well-known fight-or-flight response. It involves a surge of stress hormones like adrenaline (epinephrine) and cortisol.

In an instant, your heart rate shoots up, pumping blood to your muscles; your breathing quickens to supply oxygen; your blood sugar spikes to give quick energy; non-essential functions (like digestion) slow down; and you might even feel a cold sweat as your body primes to cool itself during exertion.

This is an incredible survival mechanism – it can help you react fast, hit harder, run faster, or just be more alert in a crisis.

Some people, when they cannot fight or escape, go into a **freeze** response – like a deer in headlights or playing dead. This too is a survival mechanism (some predators lose interest if you're "dead"; also freezing can sometimes make a person less detectable).

Freezing can feel like your body shutting down, you might feel paralyzed or disconnected (dissociation). These responses (fight, flight, freeze) are involuntary – they happen without conscious thought, triggered by the brain's alarm center.

During a traumatic event, these physical responses can be extreme. People often report things like trembling, heart pounding "out of my chest," feeling dizzy or nauseated (as blood leaves the stomach area), maybe even voiding bladder/bowels if terrified (the body dumping excess weight).

You might get tunnel vision or your hearing might become muffled – blood flow and attention are narrowing to focus on survival.

Time might feel slow or super fast (an effect of adrenaline on perception). All of this is the body's **acute stress response**. It usually subsides in minutes or hours after the threat passes, but it leaves a powerful imprint.

In the aftermath, many trauma survivors experience **somatic symptoms**: headaches, fatigue, muscle tension, upset stomach, jumpiness. This is partly because their bodies remain on high alert.

If PTSD develops, as we discussed, the body basically doesn't fully stand down from fight-or-flight. It's like the accelerator is stuck – even at rest, stress hormones can be higher than normal, and the relaxation response (the parasympathetic nervous system) is dampened.

This has a lot of consequences.

Chronic stress effects: Living with untreated trauma or PTSD means your body is exposed to chronic stress chemistry. Cortisol, for instance, when elevated for long periods, can contribute to all kinds of health issues: immune system suppression (making you more prone to infections), weight changes, memory impairment (cortisol affects the hippocampus), and even cardiovascular problems. Indeed, research has found that trauma survivors, especially those with PTSD, have higher rates of various physical health problems. For example:

- **Cardiovascular issues:** Higher risk of high blood pressure, heart disease, heart attacks. One reason might be the constant strain of adrenaline and cortisol on the heart and blood vessels. One study found childhood trauma was associated with increased incidence of ischemic heart disease and other chronic illnesses later.
- **Gastrointestinal problems:** Many people with trauma history have digestive troubles – like irritable bowel syndrome, stomach ulcers, or appetite disturbances. The gut is very sensitive to stress. Butterflies in your stomach are just the start; chronic stress can alter gut motility and even the gut microbiome.
- **Chronic pain:** There's a strong link between trauma and chronic pain conditions (fibromyalgia, back pain, headaches). Part of this is muscle tension – a trauma survivor might unconsciously hold their muscles tight (ready to spring) all the time, leading to pain. Also, the nervous system's pain thresholds can change under chronic stress.
- **Sleep disturbances:** We mentioned insomnia as a PTSD symptom. Poor sleep itself has a cascade of negative effects on health – from fatigue and cognitive impairment to increased risk for diabetes and obesity.
- **Immune and inflammation:** Ongoing stress can dysregulate the immune system, sometimes causing increased inflammation in the body. This might help explain links to conditions like arthritis or other autoimmune issues – though research is ongoing, some studies show trauma survivors have higher markers of inflammation.
- **Risky behaviors impact:** Sometimes trauma leads people to smoke, drink, or overeat as coping. These behaviors obviously can harm health (leading to liver problems, lung disease, etc.). Some of the health risk associated with PTSD is due to such behaviors as well.

To be clear, ***not every trauma survivor will get all or any of these issues.*** But statistically, a lifetime of traumatic stress can increase the likelihood of various health problems. The landmark ***ACE (Adverse Childhood***

Experiences) study found that the more trauma a person had as a child (like abuse, neglect, household dysfunction), the higher their risk for things like heart disease, cancer, diabetes, and even a shorter lifespan.

Trauma is literally hard on the heart (both figuratively and literally).

Another interesting angle: trauma can become "stored" in the body in specific ways. For example, people who have experienced sexual abuse or assault may later develop chronic pelvic pain or unexplained gynecological issues. Those with whiplash from a car accident might later have chronic neck tension that also flares when emotionally stressed.

The mind-body connection means emotional trauma can manifest as physical symptoms – sometimes called **psychosomatic symptoms**. This does not mean "faking"; it's a real physical reaction, just triggered by psychological factors. For instance, anxiety might cause real chest pain even if your heart is fine, because the muscles and nerves there are activated by stress.

The Body's Memory: Have you ever had a physical reaction that surprised you? Perhaps your heart started racing out of nowhere, or you suddenly felt sick when walking into a certain building, before your mind even realized why. The body can carry implicit memories of trauma.

Maybe the scent of a cologne causes your shoulders to tense (because a perpetrator wore that scent), even if you haven't consciously made that connection. We sometimes find that during trauma therapy, when a person starts talking about the trauma, they feel it in their body – maybe chest tightness, or their hands get cold, or they shake.

That's the body re-experiencing aspects of the event. This is why some treatment approaches specifically involve the body (we'll discuss **somatic therapies** later, which leverage bodily awareness and release).

On the flip side, recovery from trauma often involves **healing the body** too. This means learning ways to calm the physical stress response. Techniques like deep breathing, relaxation exercises, yoga, and other mind-body practices directly target the physiology of trauma.

For example, **deep belly breathing** activates the vagus nerve, which can lower heart rate and promote the relaxation response, counteracting the fight-or-flight state. Many trauma survivors find that physical activities help them release tension – whether it's exercise, dance, or even punching a pillow in a safe context. Emotions are tightly linked to physical state (think of how anger might make your body feel hot or tense, while calm contentment feels loose and warm). So part of healing is retraining the body to feel safe again.

There's also an aspect of **body ownership**. People who have been physically or sexually violated often feel a disconnect or hatred toward their own body afterward. They might think "*My body betrayed me*" or just want to numb any sensations. Reconnecting gently with one's body – through safe touch, relaxation, or movement – is an important piece of healing. It can be as simple as learning to notice bodily sensations without fear again (*"I notice my heart beating fast; that's okay, it will slow down. I am safe now.*").

Let's not forget, trauma can also result in **immediate physical injuries** if it involves violence or accidents. Those injuries (burns, wounds, broken bones) may heal, but they can leave chronic pain or disabilities that themselves are traumatic.

Managing those is part of recovery too. Sometimes, even old injuries will flare up when one is emotionally triggered, due to muscle memory or stress-induced inflammation.

Before we conclude this chapter, it's worth mentioning **professional help for bodily issues**: If you suffer from chronic pain, headaches, stomach issues, etc., it's wise to get a medical evaluation.

It's not always trauma-related of course – so rule out medical conditions. But if nothing medical explains it, consider that trauma/stress might be contributing. Treatments like physiotherapy, pain management programs, or integrative medicine approaches (acupuncture, biofeedback) can complement psychological trauma therapy.

Bottom line: Trauma puts the body through the wringer, both during the event and potentially long after. PTSD is not just "in the mind" – it's whole-body. Your racing heart, tense muscles, dizziness, fatigue, or gut problems might all be tied into the trauma you endured. This is validating (you're not imagining it – your body really is reacting) but also challenging (because it can feel like there's no escape even in your own body). The path to recovery will involve teaching your body that it doesn't have to be on red alert all the time. It involves learning to soothe your nervous system and slowly release the pent-up energy of fight/flight that might be locked inside.

REFLECTION EXERCISE: SCANNING YOUR BODY

Let's do a quick check-in.

How is your body feeling right now as you read this? Take a moment to notice from head to toe. Are your shoulders tight? Is your jaw clenched or relaxed? How is your breathing – shallow or deep? Do you notice any aches or sensations anywhere?

____
____
____
____
____
____
____

____
____
____
____
____
____
____

Often we go about our day disconnected from our bodies unless something really hurts. But building awareness is the first step to addressing physical stress.

If you detect tension (say in your neck or back), try doing a gentle stretch or just shrug and then relax your shoulders.

If you notice your breathing is shallow, try taking a slow, deep breath, filling your belly, and exhale slowly. See if that changes how you feel.

This kind of body scan and adjustment can be done regularly to help release stress bit by bit.

In upcoming chapters on coping and therapies, we will highlight specific techniques (like relaxation exercises, mindful movement, etc.) to help with the physical side of trauma.

For now, just keep in mind that your body might speak the language of trauma (through pain or tension), and it needs care and healing just as your mind does.

CHAPTER 5: EMOTIONAL AND BEHAVIORAL EFFECTS OF TRAUMA

Trauma doesn't only cause PTSD symptoms – it can also lead to broader **emotional and behavioral changes**. Survivors often say "*I didn't recognize myself after it happened.*"

This chapter explores those changes: the shifts in mood, personality, and behavior that can come in trauma's wake. Some of these overlap with PTSD criteria we already covered (like anger, guilt, avoidance), but here we'll expand beyond the diagnostic checklist to paint a fuller picture of a trauma survivor's inner world and outward actions. Understanding these effects can help survivors be kinder to themselves ("*it makes sense I feel this way, given what I went through*") and help their loved ones be more patient and supportive.

Emotional aftermath: Imagine your emotional life as a palette of colors. Trauma can throw a huge bucket of one color over everything – often that color is fear or sadness – making it hard to see the other hues.

Many trauma survivors experience intense **anxiety** – a constant sense of dread or worry that something bad will happen again.

They might also feel deep **sadness or depression**, especially if the trauma involved loss (loss of loved ones, loss of one's pre-trauma life, loss of safety). There can be profound **grief** for what or who was lost. **Anger** is another common emotion – anger at the perpetrator (if there was one), at fate, at the people who didn't help, or just a free-floating rage at the injustice of it all. Sometimes this anger is misdirected at loved ones or oneself.

A particularly challenging emotion is **guilt or shame**. Trauma survivors often blame themselves, even when it's objectively not their fault. A sexual assault survivor might think "*I shouldn't have gone out that night*," a combat veteran might feel guilt over surviving when others didn't (survivor's guilt), or someone who lived through an accident might be ashamed of how they behaved during it ("*I froze, I'm such a coward*"). These self-critical thoughts can be very painful and hard to shake. In reality, these reactions (freezing, surviving) are not moral failings – they are what people do under extreme stress.

Part of recovery is gently confronting and easing these unwarranted guilt and shame feelings.

Trust and relationships: Emotionally, trauma often **shatters trust**. If you were harmed by another person, you may come to see all people as potential threats. Even if the trauma was impersonal (like a natural disaster), you might feel that the world is unpredictable and unsafe, which can make you withdraw from others.

It's common for survivors to pull away from friends or family, either because they don't feel anything and can't connect, or because they fear being hurt or not understood.

You might feel **lonely** yet also unable to reach out. Conversely, some trauma survivors desperately cling to loved ones out of fear of being alone or unsafe – this can come across as dependent or anxious attachment.

Trauma can thus put a strain on relationships: you might lose your temper more, or conversely become so numb that you seem distant. Loved ones might not comprehend these changes and take them personally ("*she doesn't love me anymore*" or "*he's always angry at me*"), when in fact it's the trauma's fallout.

Behavioral changes: Trauma can lead to noticeable changes in behavior and lifestyle. One common pattern is **avoidance behavior**, as we covered. This could mean avoiding not just trauma reminders but any situation that feels even remotely threatening.

For example, someone assaulted at night might stop going out after dark entirely; a veteran with PTSD might avoid crowds and sit facing the door in any restaurant (hypervigilance behavior). Over time, this avoidance can shrink one's life activities significantly.

Another behavioral effect is the development of **coping mechanisms**, some healthy and some not. On the unhealthy side, many trauma survivors turn to **substance use** (alcohol, drugs) to numb their feelings or sleep.

It's estimated a large percentage of people with PTSD also have substance abuse issues as a result. Others might engage in **self-harm** (like cutting) as a way to convert emotional pain into physical pain, or to feel something when they're numb.

Risky behaviors – *driving recklessly, getting into fights, promiscuity without care for safety* – can also increase (sometimes termed "reckless self-soothing" or a search for feeling alive). These behaviors can be dangerous and create new problems (legal issues, injuries, etc.), so addressing them is often a part of trauma treatment.

On the more positive side, some survivors find constructive outlets: throwing themselves into work or a cause (which can be healing but also can be a form of avoidance if taken to extremes), exercising a lot (physical release of stress), or *channeling pain into art or writing*.

We'll talk more about healthy coping in the next chapter. Here, it's important to note that trauma often disrupts prior routines. Someone who was punctual and organized might become erratic and miss work due to insomnia or depression. Academic or job performance might drop.

Self-care can decline; for instance, a depressed trauma survivor might neglect their hygiene or health appointments. Been there? You might want to save that answer for later.

Sense of self: Perhaps one of the most profound effects is how trauma can change the way you see yourself, known as your **self-concept**.

People often go from seeing themselves as generally competent or good, to feeling damaged, broken, weak, dirty, guilty, or otherwise negative after trauma. A confident person might now be riddled with self-doubt. Someone who felt in control of their life might now feel utterly helpless or ineffective.

This erosion of self-esteem is like a secondary wound inflicted by trauma. It's not justified, but it is common – trauma can make anyone feel small and vulnerable. Regaining a positive (and realistic) sense of self is a crucial part of recovery.

Worldview shifts: Similarly, beliefs about the world and others can shift drastically. Prior to trauma, you might believe "people are generally good" or "bad things won't happen if I'm careful." Trauma can shatter those assumptions, leaving beliefs like "the world is completely unsafe," "nobody can be trusted," or "God abandoned me." Such sweeping worldview changes often underlie the symptoms of PTSD and depression. They can also be part of what needs healing – learning to develop a more balanced view (e.g., "*bad things happen, but there is still goodness and safety in parts of the world*" or "*some people can be trusted, even if others can't*").

Stigma and isolation: We also have to consider the external environment's effect on the survivor's emotions and behavior. Unfortunately, there is still **stigma** around trauma and mental health in many communities. A survivor might feel ashamed to talk about what happened, or fear that others will judge them ("you're weak for having PTSD" or "it's your fault for being there").

In some cultures, seeking therapy or talking to strangers (like a counselor) is frowned upon. This stigma can cause survivors to hide their struggles, which can worsen their mental state and lead to more withdrawal or even secret self-medication.

It's so important to break that silence. One of the goals of this book, and trauma-informed care in general, is to say: There is no shame in struggling after trauma. It is a common human reaction, and help is available.

Potential for growth: Not all emotional changes from trauma are negative. Some people, after healing some, report that they developed new strengths – perhaps they are more empathetic to others' suffering, or they value life more, or they discovered their own resilience. This is often referred to as **post-traumatic growth**.

It's not universal and it certainly doesn't mean trauma is a "good" thing (nobody needs trauma to grow!). But it's heartening that many survivors eventually find meaning in their journey – like turning their pain into a purpose (for example, volunteering, writing, or just living more authentically).

We'll delve more into growth in the concluding chapters, but I mention it here to plant a seed of hope: your emotional landscape can not only recover but possibly become richer in some ways.

For now, let's recap how trauma can affect emotions and behavior in day-to-day life:

- **Persistent fear/anxiety:** Feeling on edge, easilyscared, worried about safety constantly.
- **Depression and grief:** Deep sadness, loss of interest in life, crying spells, or numbness.
- **Anger and irritability:** Quick to anger, feeling rage about what happened or general anger at the world, sometimes leading to aggressive behavior or lashing out.
- **Guilt and shame:** Blaming oneself for the trauma or outcomes, feeling ashamed of being "weak" or of things one had to do to survive.
- **Social withdrawal or clinginess:** Either isolating oneself from friends/family, or becoming very dependent due to fear of being alone.
- **Avoidance behaviors:** Staying away from certain places/activities, or general disengagement from life to avoid triggers.
- **Risky or self-destructive behaviors:** Substance abuse, self-harm, reckless driving, unprotected sex, overeating or not eating, etc., as ways to cope or feel.
- **Changes in self-perception:** Viewing oneself as broken, bad, helpless, or permanently altered in a negative way.

- **Distrust of others:** Difficulty in relationships, assuming others will hurt or not understand you.
- **Loss of beliefs:** If you had strong religious or philosophical beliefs, trauma can shake or shatter them (or in some cases strengthen them – it varies).

- **Work or school problems:** Trouble concentrating, staying motivated, meeting responsibilities, perhaps due to symptoms or lack of sleep.
- **Stuck in survival mode:** Many of these behaviors are really just attempts to survive emotionally (even if they appear maladaptive on the outside).

If you recognize these things in yourself or someone you love, it's important to realize they are common responses to trauma.

They are not a sign of being "crazy" or bad. Understanding this can be the first step to changing them. For example, once you realize that your angry outbursts stem from a hair-trigger fight response because you're constantly anxious, you can start practicing techniques to soothe that anxiety (so the anger doesn't ignite so fast). Or if you realize you're drinking every night because you can't sleep due to nightmares, that can motivate you to seek trauma-focused therapy to resolve those nightmares rather than continuing a damaging coping strategy.

In the next chapter, we will shift into **healing frameworks and coping strategies**. That's the hopeful side: what you can actively do to start feeling better and regain control of your life.

As a bridge, let's include an exercise here for reflecting on your emotions and perhaps expressing them safely:

The Feel Wheel

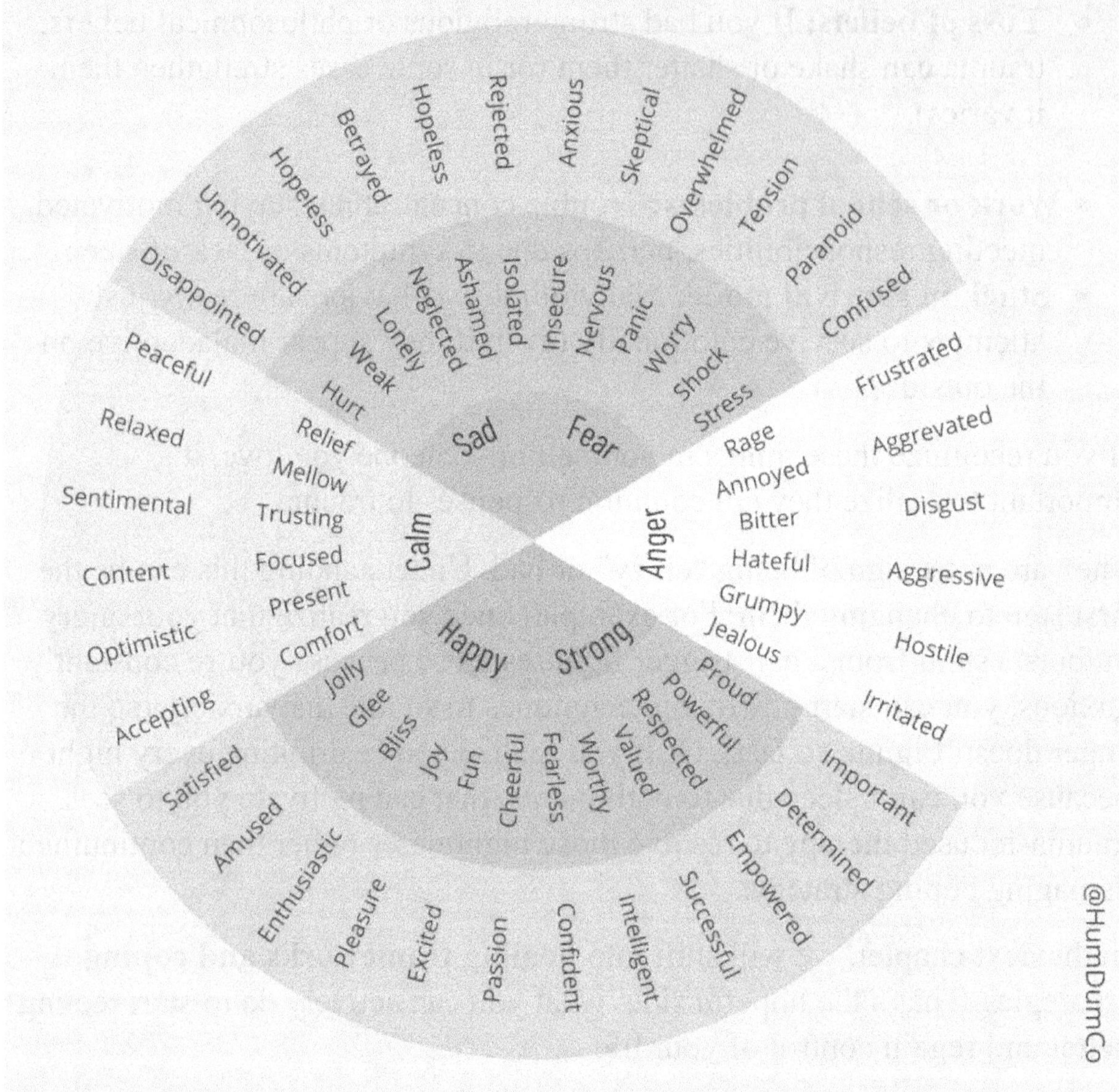

JOURNALING EXERCISE: NAMING YOUR FEELINGS

Sometimes feelings after trauma are so jumbled that it's hard to even know what we're feeling. A helpful step can be to **name and acknowledge** the emotions inside you, without judgment. This exercise will use journaling (writing) as a tool. If you're not a fan of writing, you can also just think about it or speak out loud when alone.

Take a piece of paper or your journal. You can refer to The Feel Wheel to give name to your feelings.

Write down the prompt: "***Since the trauma, I often feel…***" and then just let yourself list whatever feelings come to mind.

Don't overthink it.

You might write, for example: "***I often feel angry. I feel afraid. I feel numb. I feel guilty. I feel lonely. I feel unsafe. I feel unworthy...***" – whatever fits.

Try to be honest with yourself. Nobody else has to see this, so be truthful.

After listing the feelings, look at each word you wrote. For each one, write a brief note about **why** you think you feel that or what tends to trigger it.

For example: "*Angry – because it feels so unfair that this happened / because people don't understand me now.*"

"***Afraid – I don't feel safe going out anymore.***"

"***Guilty – I keep thinking I should have done X differently***," and so on.

This part helps connect the emotion to context.

Now, read it over and then write one more sentence:

"These feelings are valid, given what I went through."

You might feel awkward writing that, but it's an affirmation. It doesn't mean you'll feel this way forever, but it acknowledges that it makes sense to have these emotions. You have been through a lot.

Lastly, write:

"I am feeling these, but they do not define me. I am more than my trauma."

This is to remind yourself (and literally see on paper) that while trauma impacts you, it is not the sum total of you. There might be other emotions too – maybe hope, determination, love – still in you.

Journaling like this can externalize the tangle of feelings. It helps some people reduce the overwhelm, because instead of a fog of distress, you now see "*okay, I have specific feelings and reasons.*"

It's the beginning of making sense of the emotional chaos. If any of the feelings you wrote are especially intense or concerning (say, suicidal came up, or completely hopeless), make a note to mention that to a therapist or doctor. Those are signs you could use some extra support right now – and that's perfectly okay.

Keep this journal entry. Later, after doing some coping techniques or therapy, you might revisit it and see if any feelings have shifted. It's a way to track progress in the healing journey.

Next, let's talk about those healing strategies and frameworks – how do we go from living in trauma's shadow to stepping into the light of recovery?

CHAPTER 6: RECOGNIZING TRAUMA AND PTSD IN YOURSELF AND OTHERS

(**Important for Readers**: *If you've experienced trauma, you may recognize these signs. This information can validate your experiences and help you identify previously unnoticed related symptoms.*

Guidance for Supporters: *If you're here to understand a loved one's experience, this will help you identify potential indicators and gain insight into what they might be going through.*)

Identifying trauma's effects is a crucial step toward healing.

Often people suffer symptoms for a long time without realizing it's related to past trauma. They might think *"I'm just irritable and can't sleep, I don't know why"* or a child might be misdiagnosed with behavior problems when in fact they're reacting to trauma.

In this chapter, We'll try to outline what to look for – the **signs of trauma and PTSD** – across different ages and contexts.

We'll also touch on the concept of "trauma triggers" and how to recognize them.

In Yourself: How Do You Know If You Are Dealing With Trauma Or PTSD?

Some questions to ask:

1. Did you experience or witness something life-threatening, terrifying, or deeply distressing (recently or in the past)?
2. Since then, have you felt **different** than before? For example, more on edge, more sad, less trusting, unable to enjoy things?
3. Do you have **intrusive memories or nightmares** about it that bother you unexpectedly?
4. Do you ever feel or act as if the event is happening again (for instance, panicking at a similar situation)?
5. Are you going out of your way to **avoid** things that remind you of it (people, places, conversations)?
6. Has your **sleep or concentration** significantly worsened?
7. Are you more **jumpy or irritable** than you used to be?
8. Do you feel **detached** from people, or like you can't feel positive emotions?
9. Do you have **physical symptoms** like aches, fatigue, or immune issues that started after the trauma?

If you answered yes to many of these (more than 5), it's a strong indication that you are dealing with post-traumatic stress. You don't have to self-diagnose; a mental health professional can do a proper assessment for you.

But self-awareness is key.

Some survivors minimize their suffering – "*Others went through worse, I should be fine*" – and therefore don't seek help.

Recognizing that what you're experiencing is valid and significant is the first step.

In Others: If You Suspect Someone You Know Might Be Struggling With Trauma, Look For

Changes In Their Behavior And Mood After A Known Adverse Event.

For example, a friend who was in an abusive relationship might now be very withdrawn and flinches at touch. Or a combat veteran relative might be having angry outbursts and drinking more, when they used to be mild-mannered.

Key signs include:

1. **Hyperarousal signs:** Does the person seem overly alert, scanning surroundings, startled by noises easily? Do they insist on being armed or always sitting facing the door? These might be trauma-related.
2. **Avoidance and isolation:** Have they stopped doing activities they used to love or avoiding specific places? Do they cancel plans more often or seem to stay home almost all the time? Avoidance is a coping mechanism for trauma.
3. **Emotional changes:** Are they more depressed, flat, or irritable? Maybe they cry more easily or conversely show less emotion than before. Trauma can numb or amplify emotions in ways that look like personality change.
4. **Telling signs in conversation:** Do they frequently mention being unable to sleep due to nightmares? Or say things like "You wouldn't understand" or "I keep seeing it when I close my eyes"? Or "I just don't feel safe anymore." Those are pretty direct clues.
5. **Self-medication:** Notice if they're using alcohol/drugs more, or other escapism like excessive gaming, as a way to cope.
6. **Stories from others:** Sometimes you hear from mutual friends or family that "Oh, ever since X happened to them, they've been different." That collective observation often points to trauma effects.

Children and Teens: Recognizing trauma in young people has its own considerations (Important to note, identifying trauma in children, specially those under 7 is difficult as a lot of emotions overlap with their milestones. Professional intervention is always recommended):

- **Young children (under ~7):** Look for regression (losing skills like bedwetting or baby talk coming back), new separation anxiety, new fears (monsters, dark, etc.) that relate vaguely to the trauma, reenacting the trauma in play or drawings, or unexplained tantrums and clinginess. Some kids get very quiet and withdrawn instead. Physical complaints like stomach aches or headaches with no medical cause can be a child's way of expressing stress.
- **School-age children:** They might have all of the above plus trouble at school – drop in grades, difficulty paying attention, aggressive behavior or hyperactivity (which might be misdiagnosed as ADHD when it's trauma). They may talk about death or safety more. They might try to avoid school if the trauma is associated with it (e.g., bullying or an incident at school).
- **Teenagers:** Teens might resemble adults in symptoms – nightmares, avoiding reminders, mood swings. However, they might be more prone to risk-taking or acting out. Traumatized teens may engage in substance use, get into fights, or show self-harm behaviors. Conversely, some become extremely perfectionistic or controlling as a way to compensate for feeling out of control. Keep an eye on changes in friend groups, dropping out of activities they used to enjoy, or themes of despair/anger in their writings or social media; these can all be indicators.

A special note: sometimes trauma in children manifests as **re-enactment** with other kids – e.g., a child who was abused might act out sexually with peers or bully someone else. This isn't always the case, but it happens and signals that the child needs help rather than punishment.

Trauma Triggers: You'll hear the word trigger a lot in trauma discussions. A trigger is anything that reminds the person of the trauma and sets off their symptoms. Triggers can be obvious (like hearing fireworks triggering a veteran into a flashback of gunfire) or very subtle (the whiff of a cologne that a perpetrator wore, a certain time of year or day, a phrase someone uses, a particular posture of someone's body, etc.).

Part of recognizing trauma effects is identifying what triggers you or your loved one. If you notice you suddenly go from 0 to 100 in panic or anger and it's not clear why, try to backtrack – what happened just before that feeling? Perhaps a sound, smell, or situation unconsciously reminded you of the traumatic event.

For example, someone who nearly drowned might not realize why they felt anxious all day – until they recall that earlier they walked by a building with a swimming pool smelling of chlorine. Our brains often connect triggers without us realizing.

By pinpointing triggers, you can start to either avoid them strategically (though you can't avoid everything) or work with a therapist to **desensitize** them (which therapies like exposure therapy or EMDR often do).

If you're supporting someone with trauma, ask them (gently) about their triggers or just observe: maybe they get tense every time the news comes on, or they never sit in the backseat of a car anymore. Respect those triggers.

Don't force them into it ("Oh come on, you have to get over it"). Instead, help create a sense of safety. Over time, triggers can lose their power, but it requires feeling safe and possibly therapeutic intervention.

Self-assessment and Seeking Help: There are questionnaires and checklists professionals use to assess PTSD (like the PCL-5, etc.), but an informal self-check is what we've described. If you suspect trauma is affecting you or someone close, the best step is to consult a mental health professional.

They can differentiate PTSD from other issues and start appropriate treatment. Even if it's not "full PTSD," there's something called **partial**

PTSD or **acute stress disorder** that still warrants help. Don't feel you need to have every symptom severely to "qualify" for help.

If you're suffering, that's enough reason.

Breaking the silence: Recognizing trauma is sometimes tricky because people might hide their symptoms out of shame or fear. If you're noticing signs in a loved one, you might consider having a caring conversation:

"Hey, I've noticed you haven't been yourself since ***[the event]****. You seem really anxious and you don't come out anymore. I'm worried about you. Do you want to talk about it or maybe get some help? I'm here for you."* – Phrases like these, coming from a place of love and without judgment, can open a door.

The person might not open up immediately, but you've signaled that you care and noticed. Sometimes that in itself is a relief to them ("*Finally, someone sees that I'm not okay*").

For oneself, breaking silence might mean confiding in a friend, or writing on an online forum for trauma survivors, or as straightforward as making a doctor's appointment and saying "I think I might have PTSD."

It can be scary to take that step, but many people feel a weight lifted once they start acknowledging it.

You don't have to hold it all inside.

Let's say you've recognized that yes, trauma has indeed left its mark. What now? That's where the **healing frameworks and strategies** come in – which is exactly where we're heading next.

Recognizing the problem is half the battle; now we can focus on solutions and coping tools to start feeling better and reclaiming life from the grip of trauma.

Transition: Now that we've identified the problem, let's dive into how to address it. The next chapters will cover evidence-based therapies for trauma, as well as practical coping skills you can use in daily life.

Remember, knowledge is power – and you've just armed yourself with a lot of knowledge about trauma and PTSD. You're ready to move toward healing.

CHAPTER 7: THE HEALING JOURNEY – FROM SURVIVING TO THRIVING

Healing from trauma is often described as a **journey**. There's no instant cure or single "aha" moment when everything is fixed. Instead, it's a process of learning, growth, setbacks, and breakthroughs. In this chapter, we'll map out what that journey can look like. We'll talk about common stages or phases of recovery, and mindset shifts that help along the way. We'll also emphasize that healing is possible – the brain and body want to heal, given the right support, just as a cut on your skin naturally moves toward closure.

One influential trauma expert, Dr. Judith Herman, described **three stages of trauma recovery**: **Safety and Stabilization**, **Processing the Trauma**, and **Reconnection & Reintegration**.

Let's explore these in approachable terms:

1. Safety and Stabilization: This is the foundation. In the immediate aftermath of trauma (or when someone first seeks help for long standing trauma issues), the priority is to establish a sense of safety in the present and stabilize intense symptoms.

Think of it like the emergency phase in physical first aid – you stop the bleeding before you do anything else.

For emotional trauma, "stopping the bleeding" means ensuring the person is out of the traumatic situation (if it was ongoing abuse, for example, finding safety away from the abuser), and managing any crisis symptoms (like severe panic attacks, suicidal thoughts, substance detox if needed).

During this phase, a person might not even talk about the trauma much – and that's okay.

The focus is on feeling safer **now**.

This can involve:

- Grounding techniques and coping strategies to handle flashbacks or anxiety (many of which we'll cover in Chapter 10).
- Building a support network (identifying friends, family, or support groups that can be leaned on).
- Possibly starting medication if symptoms are overwhelming (for example, short-term sleep aids or anti-anxiety meds as prescribed by a doctor can help stabilize, or longer-term medications like SSRIs for PTSD may be considered).
- Establishing routines of basic self-care: eating, sleeping, exercising regularly as possible, because these regulate the body and give a sense of normalcy.
- Learning about trauma (like reading this book!) so that the survivor understands that their reactions are not "crazy" but a known response – this knowledge itself is stabilizing.

In this stage, the person and any helpers (therapist, etc.) ensure that the survivor feels grounded in the present. A lot of emphasis is on **empowerment** – giving the survivor choices and control, maybe for the first time in a while.

For example, a therapist might spend time simply teaching the client that they can say "stop" at any point in therapy if they feel uncomfortable. Regaining that sense of control is key.

Only when a person has some tools to handle distress and feels a degree of safety do they usually move to the next phase.

2. Processing the Trauma (Remembrance and Mourning): This is the stage people often think of when they imagine "trauma therapy" – talking about or otherwise processing the traumatic memories themselves. It can involve gradually recounting what happened, expressing and working through all the emotions around it (grief, anger, etc.), and making sense of it in the context of one's life story. This is typically done with a trained therapist using a specific approach (like TF-CBT, EMDR, etc., which we'll discuss soon).

The goal is to **desensitize** the person to the memories – meaning, turn them from terrifying, present-tense flashbacks into tolerable, past-tense memories that no longer have the same power. It's also to help the person **mourn** any losses (people who died, loss of innocence, loss of time, etc.) and begin to let go of guilt or irrational beliefs ("It was my fault" gets challenged and ideally transformed to "I did the best I could; the blame lies on the perpetrator").

Processing can be very intense. It doesn't happen all at once; it's often a bit by bit exposure. For example, in therapy one might start by just writing a short account of a part of the event, or doing a visualization exercise that touches the edge of the memory, then use coping skills to calm down.

Over several sessions or months, they get to the point where they can recount or remember the trauma without being overwhelmed – essentially, the trauma memory gets integrated into their life story as one part of it, not this ever-present nightmare.

During this phase, having that groundwork of safety matters because diving into trauma feelings can temporarily spike symptoms. It's like doing surgery – sometimes pain increases in the short term while cleaning out the wound, but it's for long-term healing.

Important: A person should never be forced to confront memories if they're not ready. It's a collaborative and paced process. Different therapies have different methods – some involve a lot of talking directly about it (exposure therapies), others (like EMDR) have you focus on it while doing bilateral stimulation, others (somatic therapies) have you process sensations tied to the trauma, etc. But all aim to help your brain re-file that memory into the past and reduce its emotional charge.

3. Reconnection and Reintegration: In this stage, the trauma is no longer the central focus. The person begins to rebuild their life, their relationships, their sense of self beyond the trauma. They start to discover "Who am I now, after all of this? What do I want my life to look like?"

Often it involves finding meaning. Some people might choose to engage in advocacy or helping others who went through similar experiences (though that's a personal choice, not a requirement).

Many find that they can now form closer relationships again, or return to work or school with a new perspective. The idea is that the survivor moves from identifying as a victim (in the trauma) or even a patient (in therapy) to identifying as a **survivor** or **thriver**, a whole person with a future.

In this phase, sometimes people address broader life issues that may have been on hold. For example, after dealing with rape trauma, a person might now work on dating again and what healthy intimacy means for them. Or a veteran might pursue a new career path that gives them purpose, now that their PTSD symptoms are down. It's about reintegrating into society and one's own life in a fulfilling way.

There is often an element of solidifying gains – continuing self-care routines, maybe occasionally checking in with therapy or support groups to stay on track, and being mindful of triggers or stressors so they don't sneak back up.

These stages aren't strictly linear – you might work on safety, then process some, then need to focus on safety again if something destabilizes (like a new stress in life), etc. And healing is rarely 100% complete as in "I never feel a twinge about it anymore."

Rather, it reaches a point where the trauma isn't running your life. It becomes an unfortunate memory, maybe even a sad or heavy one, but it doesn't dictate your day-to-day emotions or actions.

Personal Growth: As hinted, a beautiful thing that can happen in the reconnection phase is discovering personal growth. Survivors often say things like, "I hate that this happened, I'd never wish it on anyone, but it taught me how strong I am," or "It made me more compassionate," or "It changed my priorities in life – now I don't sweat the small stuff and I treasure every day more." This phenomenon of finding positive change through trauma is known as post-traumatic growth.

It's not universal, and no one should pressure a survivor to "find the silver lining."

But it's reassuring to know that even the darkest clouds can sometimes water the seeds of something new and good in oneself. For instance, someone who lost a loved one to violence might become an activist for peace; someone who survived a terrible injury might develop a newfound appreciation for their body and what it can still do.

Healing is not linear: It's vital to set realistic expectations. People often ask, "How long will it take?" There's no set timeline. It could be months for some, years for others. There will be ups and downs. You might have a few good weeks and then suddenly feel retraumatized by a trigger; that doesn't mean you failed, it means you're human and healing is bumpy.

Sometimes new stages of life can reawaken old trauma feelings (for example, a person abused in childhood might feel triggered again when they have their own child reach the age they were abused – this can bring stuff up that needs a bit more processing, even if they were doing well).

That's okay. It's like an onion, you peel layers. Very often it gets easier and easier, and episodes of distress become fewer, farther between, and shorter.

With solid coping skills, you can weather those episodes without losing hope.

Attitude and mindset: Here are some helpful mindsets that survivors and therapists have identified for the journey:

- **Patience:** Be patient with yourself. You might want to "just be over it" now, but it takes time. Think of it like recovering from a major surgery – you wouldn't expect to run a marathon a week after heart surgery. Emotional healing is similar.
- **Self-Compassion:** Try to treat yourself with the same kindness you would treat a friend who went through what you did. Trauma survivors often are very hard on themselves. Practice saying, "It

makes sense that I feel this way; I'm doing the best I can." Self-compassion is actually linked to better trauma recovery outcomes.

- **Hope:** Even if it's a tiny glimmer, hold on to the idea that things can improve. PTSD often tricks you into feeling hopeless, like "I'll never be normal." But people do get better – not usually 100% like nothing happened (because, truthfully, trauma is a life event that does change you), but better as in functioning, enjoying life, feeling meaning again.

- **Empowerment:** Emphasize choices and control where possible. Trauma often involves having your control taken away. In healing, you get to call the shots about what coping methods to use, when to open up, which therapist to work with, etc. Recognize your courage in facing the trauma – that's empowering too.
- **Spirituality or Meaning:** Many find strength in faith or spirituality. Some turn to prayer, meditation, or religious community for support. If you are a person of faith, you might interpret your journey in that context (e.g., as a test of faith, as a path where you rely on God for strength, etc.). If not religious, you might still seek meaning in philosophy or personal values ("I survived, so I want to make my life count in XYZ way").

  Trauma often prompts deep existential questions; grappling with those (possibly with a counselor or clergy's help if appropriate) is part of the healing journey.

- **Cultural and Personal Identity:** Lean into aspects of your identity that give you strength. Your culture might have healing rituals or community practices that help (we'll discuss cultural healing soon). Your personal identity – say, as a parent, or as an artist, or as a community member – can also be a source of motivation to heal ("I want to be the best parent I can, so I will work on my trauma for my kids' sake as well as mine").

The journey may eventually lead you to a place where you consider yourself not just a survivor, but even someone who has grown. You might still have scars (literal or figurative), but you carry them with pride or acceptance rather than shame. A wound that's healed leaves a scar – it's evidence of healing, not of weakness.

It's proof that you endured and you're still here.

In the coming chapters, we will go into the specifics of **healing frameworks** (like different therapies available) and practical **tools** to use along the way. These are like the travel gear and maps for your healing journey. You don't have to use all of them; you find what works for you. Think of therapy models as different routes up a mountain – some are steeper and direct, some are winding and gentle.

All aim for the summit of recovery. I'll help you understand each, so you can choose an approach that resonates and feels doable.

Remember: **Healing is not about forgetting or erasing the past; it's about learning to live with it in peace.** The trauma becomes a chapter in your life story, not the title of your book.

Having described the overall process of healing, the following chapter will detail evidence-based trauma therapies – the structured approaches that have facilitated recovery for numerous survivors.

CHAPTER 8: EVIDENCE-BASED THERAPIES FOR TRAUMA – PATHS TO HEALING

Therapy can be a scary word to some, but it simply means **structured help** for processing your trauma and learning to cope. There are several well-researched approaches designed specifically to treat PTSD and trauma-related problems.

In this chapter, we'll break down the big ones:

Trauma-Focused Cognitive Behavioral Therapy (TF-CBT),

EMDR (Eye Movement Desensitization and Reprocessing),

Acceptance and Commitment Therapy (ACT),

Somatic Therapies, and the broader concept of **trauma-informed care** (which applies to any therapeutic relationship).

Each has its unique techniques, but they share the same goal: to help you heal in a safe, effective way. We'll describe each in an accessible manner so you can understand what they involve and how they might help.

TRAUMA-FOCUSED COGNITIVE BEHAVIORAL THERAPY (TF-CBT)

As the name implies, TF-CBT is a form of Cognitive Behavioral Therapy adapted for trauma. CBT is a widely used therapy that focuses on the connections between thoughts, feelings, and behaviors. TF-CBT specifically targets those that stem from traumatic experiences. It was originally developed for children and adolescents who had gone through abuse or other trauma, often involving their non-offending caregivers in treatment. Over time, it's been adapted for adults as well, but its core use is with younger people.

How TF-CBT works: The therapy typically lasts around 12–16 sessions (short-term), though it can be longer if needed. It's structured and has several components often remembered by the acronym **PRACTICE**:

- **P** – **Psychoeducation**: The therapist educates the client (and parent, if it's a child) about trauma and common reactions. This helps normalize the child's feelings ("I'm not the only one who has nightmares after something bad").

- **R** – **Relaxation**: They teach relaxation skills, such as deep breathing or muscle relaxation, to manage anxiety.
- **A** – **Affective modulation**: Basically, emotion regulation skills – identifying feelings, learning safe ways to express and cope with them (could include journaling, drawing feelings, etc.).
- **C** – **Cognitive coping**: This is where cognitive therapy comes in. They help the person recognize unhelpful thoughts (like "It was my fault" or "I'm permanently broken") and challenge or reframe them.

For instance, a child might learn to replace "It happened because I was bad" with "It happened because the adult made a bad choice – it's not my fault."

- **T – Trauma narrative**: This is the heart of it – the child (or adult client) gradually tells the story of what happened, in a safe and controlled way, often first by writing or drawing it, then sharing with the therapist.

They process the details, the worst moments, etc., at a pace that doesn't overwhelm. The idea is to **confront the memory in a safe environment** so it loses its terror. The therapist provides lots of support and helps challenge any distorted ideas that come up in the telling ("You keep saying you should have fought back – let's talk about how little and scared you were, and how it's really the adult who's to blame.").

- **I – In vivo mastery**: If the client is avoiding specific reminders of the trauma (like a place or activity), the therapist may do gradual exposure to those in real life once they're ready. For example, if a child was bitten by a dog and avoids all dogs, the therapist might eventually help them approach a friendly dog step by step (never forcing, but encouraging as they build courage).
- **C – Conjoint sessions**: For kids, this means some sessions are together with the parent/caregiver, so the child can share their trauma narrative with the parent (if appropriate) and the parent can learn how to best support the child. It's about improving communication and trust. For adults, "conjoint" might not apply unless involving a spouse or so, but often with adults, therapy is individual.
- **E – Enhancing safety & future development**: Towards the end, the therapist and client focus on wrapping up by ensuring the client has a safety plan (how to handle future potential dangers or triggers) and skills to thrive going forward (like good touch/bad touch education for kids to prevent future abuse, or self-care plans for adults).

TF-CBT has a **strong evidence base**, especially in reducing PTSD symptoms in children and teens. Studies find that kids treated with TF-CBT do better than those in supportive counseling alone, often showing significant drops in anxiety, depression, shame, and behavioral problems. It's considered a gold standard for youth trauma by many organizations.

For adults, the principles are similar (though you wouldn't involve a parent, obviously). A trauma-focused CBT for adults might be very similar to a treatment called **Cognitive Processing Therapy (CPT)** or **Prolonged Exposure (PE)**, which are offshoots of CBT for trauma. CPT emphasizes writing about the trauma and challenging thoughts; PE emphasizes repeatedly talking through the trauma memory and facing avoided triggers. TF-CBT is like a blend of these, plus the coping skill work.

What it feels like as a client: In TF-CBT, you'd typically start by building trust with the therapist, learning those coping skills (so you feel equipped to handle the tough parts), and only once you feel ready, you start discussing the trauma in detail. The therapist is very attuned to not pushing you too fast.

They may give homework, like practicing a relaxation exercise at home, or writing a part of your story. It's a collaborative, gentle process, but also direct in addressing the trauma (no "skirting around the issue" once you're in the narrative phase). Many people find it challenging but ultimately relieving – finally talking about it openly can lift a burden of silence and secrecy.

In cases with kids, involving the parent (if the parent is safe/supportive) helps the child see that their caregiver hears what happened and still loves and accepts them; it's very healing for the parent to express that and for the child to feel not alone.

Special notes: TF-CBT is suitable for a wide range of traumas – abuse, domestic violence exposure, disaster, etc. It's typically not used if the trauma is still ongoing (for instance, if a child is still in an abusive situation, the focus first would be on getting them safe; processing might come once they're safe). It can be adapted for different cultures and has been used globally. If you're a parent reading this and your child went through something terrible, seeking a therapist trained in TF-CBT is a good step. The therapist will work with you too, so you can help your child.

Eye Movement Desensitization and Reprocessing (EMDR)

EMDR is one of the most intriguing trauma therapies out there. It was developed by Francine Shapiro in the late 1980s. At first glance, it sounds a bit odd: it involves the client focusing on trauma memories while simultaneously moving their eyes back and forth (following the therapist's finger or a light), or sometimes tapping or other bilateral stimulation. But it's far from hocus-pocus – it's now an extensively researched, mainstream treatment for PTSD recommended by organizations like the WHO and Department of Veterans Affairs.

How EMDR works: The theory behind EMDR is that traumatic memories sometimes don't get properly "processed" by the brain; they're stuck in a raw, upsetting form. Engaging in bilateral stimulation (left-right eye movement or tapping) while recalling the trauma is thought to help the brain process and integrate the memory, similar to what happens naturally during REM sleep (when your eyes move back and forth and your brain is processing memories). Whether that exact mechanism is correct or not, research shows EMDR is effective in reducing trauma symptoms. Interestingly, some studies suggest that the eye movements themselves aren't magic by themselves but that the exposure + dual attention aspect is key – but there's debate. What's important is, it works about as well as other trauma-focused therapies like TF-CBT/PE.

What an EMDR session looks like: In EMDR, like other therapies, there's an initial phase of ensuring the client has some stabilization skills (they teach you a "safe/calm place" visualization, for example, to use if you get overwhelmed). Then you identify a target memory to work on.

Let's say someone has an assault memory that's haunting them. The therapist will ask the client to bring up that memory in their mind – including the image that disturbs them most, the negative belief about self that goes with it ("I'm powerless" or "I'm dirty" for example), and notice what emotions and body sensations come. Then, while the client holds that in mind, the therapist will start a series of bilateral stimulation – typically moving their finger left-right and having the client track it with their eyes, for maybe 30 seconds to a minute.

Then they stop and ask, “What do you notice now?” The client might say, “I feel really angry thinking about it.” The therapist says, “Go with that,” and does another set of eye movements. They continue in sets like this. The client’s thoughts might shift – they might go from anger to sadness to some insight like “It wasn’t my fault.” The therapist doesn’t guide these changes so much as facilitate them; your brain sort of processes on its own with the dual attention.

They continue until that memory doesn’t feel so upsetting anymore – ideally the client can think of it and say, “It happened, it’s over, and I believe now that I’m not to blame and I’m safe.” They install a positive belief (“I am strong” or “I am in control now”) with the eye movements as well, to kind of cement a healthier perspective. They also do a scan to check if your body still reacts (like if you still feel tension when thinking of it; if so, they target that sensation).

One hallmark of EMDR is you don’t have to describe the memory in detail out loud if you don’t want to – you just have to hold it in mind. For people who dread talking about trauma, this is appealing. The therapist will ask you what you’re noticing, but you don’t necessarily narrate the whole story. Some do share bits, but it’s less of a conversation than CBT-based therapy.

Does EMDR really work?: Yes, for many people. Numerous studies have shown it reduces PTSD symptoms, often fairly quickly. It’s endorsed by many international guidelines (WHO, etc.). However, how it works is somewhat controversial – some believe the eye movements are crucial, others think it’s just another form of exposure therapy with a distraction element (the dual attention). Shapiro argued that it taps into the brain’s adaptive processing.

Regardless, clients often report after EMDR that the traumatic memory feels more distant, like it happened a long time ago, or that it no longer sparks intense emotion – it becomes a neutral memory. They might also have new insights (“I realize now I did the best I could” or “I see now that I’m safe in the present”). EMDR also often addresses multiple memories or the “root” memory of a pattern. For example, they might process an early childhood trauma that is linked to current relationship triggers.

What it feels like: Some people feel EMDR is less emotionally draining than prolonged exposure therapy, because you’re not verbally describing the trauma over and over. Others still find it emotional but in a different way – some cry during it, some are exhausted after (processing in the brain can be tiring). Often clients like that they see progress in a concrete way: a memory that was 10/10 distress might come down to 1/10 after a few sessions on it.

It can feel weird at first (following a finger with your eyes while thinking of something painful is unusual!), but therapists do it in a very supportive way. There’s also tapping or auditory beeps as alternatives to eye movements for those who can’t or don’t want the eye stuff.

EMDR can be used for single-incident trauma or complex trauma, though complex trauma might require a longer preparation phase and many targets. It’s also been used for things like phobias or grief with some success.

In summary, EMDR **“re-processes” trauma memories** in a way that helps the brain file them correctly. It’s widely recognized as effective for PTSD, though not everyone chooses it. It’s one of the options, and many people who try it are surprised at how such a simple-sounding thing (eye movements) can help – but the key is it’s done within a comprehensive therapeutic approach (with safety, titration of exposure, etc.).

Acceptance and Commitment Therapy (ACT)

Acceptance and Commitment Therapy is a newer (so-called "third wave") behavior therapy that isn't specific to trauma, but it has been applied to trauma and PTSD with good results. The premise of ACT is a bit different: it doesn't focus on reducing symptoms per se or processing the content of trauma directly, but rather on changing one's relationship to thoughts and feelings. The name gives it away – Acceptance of what is out of your control (like past trauma, or persistent thoughts) and Commitment to taking action guided by your values.

In simpler terms, ACT helps you learn to **accept painful emotions and thoughts** instead of constantly fighting them, and to focus on living a meaningful life even with some pain. For trauma survivors who feel consumed by memories or anxiety, ACT can teach skills to not let that consumption happen.

Key components of ACT:

- **Mindfulness:** ACT training involves a lot of mindfulness – learning to observe your thoughts and feelings without judgment, almost like watching clouds pass in the sky. You learn that you are not your thoughts; you have thoughts. For example, instead of "It's hopeless, I'll never get better" (and buying into that), you notice "I'm having the thought that it's hopeless". This little shift creates distance. You don't necessarily try to argue the thought away (like CBT would); you just see it as a thought, not a literal truth you have to obey.
- **Acceptance:** This means making room for feelings instead of resisting them. If anxiety comes, instead of thinking "No no I can't feel this!", you practice accepting "Here is anxiety, I can allow it to be present," perhaps using breathing or mindfulness to ride the wave. It's like the idea "what you resist, persists." By accepting, strangely, the feelings often move on more quickly or at least bother you less.
- **Defusion:** That's the term ACT uses for what I described about thoughts – cognitive defusion means separating (defusing) from your

thoughts. Techniques include literally saying "I'm having the thought that X" or imagining the thought in a funny voice, or as words on a karaoke bouncing ball – anything to see it just as words, not as Reality with a capital R.

- **Values:** ACT puts a big emphasis on clarifying your values – what truly matters to you (family? creativity? honesty? helping others? achievement? etc.) – and then **committing** to actions that move you toward those, even if you have some painful feelings along the way. For example, a veteran with PTSD might deeply value being a loving parent. PTSD makes him want to avoid school events (crowds trigger him).

  In ACT, he might accept "Yes, I have anxiety in crowds and I value my child's happiness, so I will practice my mindfulness and go to that school play despite the anxiety, because being the dad I want to be is worth it." It's not pushing in an unsafe way, it's choosing meaning over avoidance.

- **Self-as-context:** A bit abstract, but ACT tries to cultivate a sense that you are more than your experiences – like there's a part of you (the observing self) that is unchanged and can witness everything. This is a bit like some spiritual teachings or meditation traditions. It can help trauma survivors not define themselves solely by the trauma ("I am not just a victim; I am the one noticing that I had this experience and the one who can take my life forward").

How does this help PTSD specifically? Research suggests that **psychological flexibility** – which is what ACT builds – helps people with trauma not get so stuck in avoidance or overwhelmed by memories. ACT doesn't necessarily make flashbacks stop (though sometimes they lessen as stress goes down), but it changes how you handle them.

You learn you can have a memory or panic attack and, rather than catastrophize, you acknowledge it and use grounding, and continue your day according to what you planned (if possible). Over time, not fighting the symptoms ironically can reduce their intensity. Also, by focusing on values, people start re-engaging in life – maybe socializing a bit even if it causes some anxiety, or doing work or hobbies that give them a sense of purpose. This can chip away at depression and isolation that fuel PTSD.

What ACT sessions look like: There's a lot of exercises, metaphors, and experiential learning. A therapist might have you do mindfulness practices in session. They use metaphors like "Passengers on the bus" (you're the driver going toward a destination (value) and the anxious thoughts are passengers yelling – you let them be and keep driving). Or "Tug of war with a monster" (if you drop the rope – i.e., stop fighting anxiety – the monster can't tug you around as much).

Sessions involve talking about your avoidance patterns and trying new approaches. You might set goals each week that align with your values, even small steps, and come back to discuss how it went and what thoughts/feelings got in the way.

There's also a newer adaptation called **ACT for PTSD** being researched. It doesn't ask you to describe the trauma in detail; instead, you talk about how the trauma impacts your life now and what moving forward looks like.

Effectiveness: Some studies show ACT reduces PTSD symptoms and improves quality of life. It might be a good fit for those who are not ready to revisit the trauma memories directly, or who have tried exposure-based therapy and still struggle with avoidance. It's also helpful if you have a mix of issues (trauma + other emotional struggles) because ACT is trans-diagnostic.

To sum up, ACT teaches **acceptance of inner experiences and commitment to valued actions**, which can help someone not be ruled by trauma-induced fear or pain. As one Healthline article put it, ACT teaches people "how to live alongside their past experiences, rather than avoid them.". That resonates with many survivors: you can't erase the past, but you can learn to carry it in a way where it doesn't weigh you down so heavily.

Somatic (Body-Based) Therapies

We've talked about the body keeping the score of trauma; **somatic therapies** aim to release trauma by working through bodily sensation and movement. Two well-known ones are **Somatic Experiencing (SE)** and **Sensorimotor Psychotherapy**, among others (including techniques like trauma-informed yoga or martial arts).

Somatic Experiencing (SE): Developed by Peter Levine, SE posits that animals in the wild shake off trauma (literally) and complete the fight/flight responses, whereas humans often get "stuck" because our socialization or freeze response stops the natural discharge of energy.

SE therapy involves helping a person become aware of their internal physical sensations (interoception) in a safe way and gently guiding them to release tension and "unlock" the trauma held in the body.

For example, someone might notice a tightness in their chest when thinking of the trauma; the therapist might have them mindfully focus on that sensation, maybe amplify it slightly, then see how their body naturally wants to move – maybe they need to cry, or their arm feels like moving (perhaps an impulse that was suppressed during the trauma).

By allowing these processes, the theory is the body completes what it needs to (like running away energy or fight energy) and thus resets.

Somatic Experiencing sessions might include small movements, breathing, sometimes sounds.

The therapist carefully monitors that the client doesn't get overwhelmed – they might work with a sensation for a short time then back off ("pendulation" between distress and safety). The idea is to **discharge the stored survival energy** gradually.

Clients often report feeling a tremble or heat release or some wave of emotion and then relaxation as their body lets go of something. It can be subtle or sometimes quite profound. One might, say, realize their neck tension is linked to holding back a scream during trauma – releasing that tension might involve actually voicing a sound or tensing-then-relaxing those muscles while feeling the suppressed urge.

Sensorimotor Psychotherapy: This approach (by Pat Ogden) similarly integrates body awareness with therapy and also ties in cognitive meaning. It often addresses how trauma affects posture, movement, etc. For example, a victim might have a collapsed posture (a bodily expression of defeat); therapy might involve helping them experiment with more upright posture and noticing the emotional effect.

Yoga and Movement: There's growing evidence that trauma-sensitive yoga can help survivors by fostering a gentle reconnection with their bodies in a controlled way. Yoga incorporates breath and mindful movement which can calm the nervous system. Many trauma survivors find that non-verbal, body-centered practices give them relief where words fail.

Even activities like tai chi, qigong, dance, or certain martial arts (with the right, sensitive instructor) can help reclaim a sense of strength and safety in the body.

Why somatic? Many times, trauma is preverbal (happened in early childhood) or so overwhelming that talking about it doesn't fully resolve the physiological imprint. Somatic methods address trauma at that sensorimotor level.

They focus on **body memories** – like flinching, or gut clenches – and work to reset the nervous system. Research on SE is still emerging, but anecdotal success is strong. One study showed significant symptom reduction. These approaches are considered alternative or adjunct by some, but they're becoming more mainstream as part of a holistic trauma treatment (often combined with talk therapy).

What it feels like: If you do somatic therapy, don't expect a lot of digging into the story.

The therapist may ask you about the trauma just broadly but then quickly move to

"What are you noticing in your body right now as we talk about this?"

They help you track sensations. If you start dissociating (numbing out), they bring you back gently perhaps by focusing on something present (like the chair under you).

Some sessions might involve the therapist guiding you: *"Listen to your body – do you feel any impulse to move or change posture as you talk about that incident?"*

They might support you to, say, push against their hands if you feel an impulse to push (representing pushing an attacker away) in a safe simulation, allowing your body to complete that action and feel empowered.

After successful somatic work, people often feel lighter, more grounded, and more present. Nightmares or hypervigilance can decrease because the body isn't stuck in "threat mode" as much.

Trauma-Informed Care (Principles Across All Therapies)

While not a specific therapy technique, **trauma-informed care** is a framework that any healthcare provider (mental health or otherwise) should ideally follow when working with trauma survivors. It basically means the professionals **understand the impact of trauma** and create an environment that promotes healing rather than inadvertently retraumatizing.

Key principles of trauma-informed care, as outlined by SAMHSA, include:

- **Safety:** Ensuring the physical and emotional safety of the client. For example, a counselor allows the client to have control over session pacing, or a clinic makes sure the waiting area feels secure and private.
- **Trustworthiness & Transparency:** Being clear, consistent, and honest so clients can rebuild trust. The therapist might explain what they're doing and why, and admit what they don't know.
- **Peer Support:** Incorporating support from others who have lived experience. Many trauma programs include peer support groups, which helps reduce isolation.
- **Collaboration & Mutuality:** The therapist is not the "boss" ordering treatment, but a collaborator. Power differences are leveled as much as possible. The client's feedback is valued; therapy is done with them, not to them.
- **Empowerment, Voice & Choice:** Emphasizing the client's strengths and autonomy. A trauma-informed therapist will constantly give the client choices – "Would you like to try this exercise, or would you prefer we talk more first?" – to give them a sense of control. They focus on resilience ("You survived – you have strengths we can build on").
- **Cultural, Historical, and Gender Issues:** Being sensitive to and actively seeking to address cultural factors and historical trauma. This means acknowledging how trauma and healing might be viewed differently in different cultures, or how a person's identity (race,

gender, religion, etc.) plays into their trauma and recovery. It's about not using stereotypes and recognizing the client's context.

In practice, if a service is trauma-informed, you would feel respected, informed, connected, and hopeful.

They would avoid potentially triggering practices (for example, a residential center might avoid having uniformed security guards because that could trigger someone who was imprisoned; or a doctor might ask permission before touching a patient during an exam, understanding they might have touch trauma). It also means staff are trained to recognize and respond to trauma reactions appropriately.

Trauma-informed care is something to look for in any provider you deal with. If a therapist or doctor or even a teacher is trauma-informed, they will be more patient if you have anxiety, they won't say things like "get over it," and they will try to make you feel as safe as possible in that setting.

It's heartening that more and more organizations are embracing this approach – it makes a huge difference. A trauma survivor with even the best therapy techniques could be set back if treated insensitively by others in the system. The ideal is a whole environment that fosters healing.

Choosing a Therapy: With all these options – TF-CBT, EMDR, ACT, somatic, etc. – how do you choose? There's no one-size-fits-all. Some people resonate with one approach over another.

If you hate talking about details, you might lean toward EMDR or ACT.

If you want a structured step-by-step proven program and like the idea of working through a trauma story gradually, TF-CBT/CPT/PE might suit you.

If you feel disconnected from your body or have lots of physical tension, a somatic approach or yoga might be wonderful (often as an adjunct to another therapy).

Many therapists are **integrative** – they use bits of multiple approaches tailored to you.

The most important factor is often the **therapeutic relationship** – you need to feel safe and understood by the therapist. A caring therapist can make any approach more effective.

So when seeking therapy, consider interviewing a couple therapists to see who you click with. Ask if they have experience with trauma and what methods they use. Good trauma therapists won't be offended by questions; they'll appreciate that you're taking an active role.

And remember, therapy is not something done to you – you're an active participant. Therapies like these often give homework or practices to do between sessions. The more you engage, the more you'll get out of it.

But also, everyone goes at their own pace. It's okay if some weeks you make great strides and others you feel stuck. The therapist is your ally through those ups and downs.

In the next chapter, we'll shift gears a bit to practical **coping strategies and self-care tools** you can use on your own.

These are things you can start right away, even if you're not in formal therapy, to manage symptoms and improve your daily functioning. In fact, many are taught within the therapies we just discussed (like relaxation in TF-CBT, or mindfulness in ACT). We gather them here in one place as a handy toolkit.

Before we move on, take a moment to reflect: How do you feel about the idea of therapy now that you have some info? Does one approach intrigue you? It's okay if it still feels daunting – a lot of people are anxious about starting therapy (ironically, talking about trauma can feel as scary as the trauma at first).

But knowledge is power. You now know these treatments exist and that PTSD is treatable.

Many people have gotten better with these methods. You have options and you have hope.

It can be overwhelming to process this information, so I have aimed to simplify it.

I recognize the societal stigma surrounding therapy, which unfortunately hinders community well-being.

The following chapter will explore accessible coping mechanisms that can be used anywhere and at any time.

These tools can enhance the benefits of therapy or provide support while awaiting professional help.

CHAPTER 9: TOOLS AND COPING STRATEGIES FOR RECOVERY

Healing from trauma isn't just about what happens in the therapist's office. **What you do day-to-day to cope and care for yourself** is equally important.

In this chapter, we compile a toolbox of practical strategies you can start using immediately.

These tools help manage stress, reduce anxiety, ground you during flashbacks or dissociation, and improve overall resilience.

Think of them as your first aid kit for trauma symptoms. We'll cover techniques like deep breathing, relaxation methods, grounding exercises, mindfulness, self-soothing, journaling, and more.

I'll also talk about lifestyle factors – sleep, exercise, nutrition – and the role of social support.

By the end of this, you might want to pick a few strategies to practice, making them part of your routine.

It's a good idea to try different tools and see what resonates.

Not every strategy works for everyone, but **many survivors find these make a huge difference** in regaining a sense of control and calming their minds and bodies when trauma symptoms flare up.

Breathing and Relaxation Techniques

One of the simplest yet most powerful tools is your **breath**. When we're anxious or triggered, our breathing often becomes rapid and shallow (from the chest). By consciously slowing and deepening your breathing, you send a signal to your nervous system that it's okay to calm down. Here are two core techniques:

- **Deep Diaphragmatic Breathing:** Also known as belly breathing.
  - To practice, sit or lie comfortably.
  - Place one hand on your belly. Inhale slowly through your nose to a count of about 4, feeling your belly push out (imagine filling your stomach with air).
  - This means you're using your diaphragm fully.
  - Then exhale gently through your mouth for a count of 6 (or longer than the inhale), feeling your belly fall.
  - Try to make the exhale a little longer than the inhale; this especially triggers relaxation.
  - As you breathe, focus on the sound and feeling of the breath. If you like, you can say a word like "calm" or "safe" to yourself on each exhale.
  - Repeat for a few minutes. Deep breathing like this can reduce the physical signs of stress (heart rate, blood pressure) and help during anxious moments or when trying to sleep.
  - It might feel a bit odd if you're not used to belly breathing – many of us habitually breathe shallowly. With practice, it gets easier and more automatic. Think of this as resetting your system.
- **Progressive Muscle Relaxation (PMR):** Trauma often keeps us in a tense state without realizing it. PMR is an exercise where you systematically tense and then relax different muscle groups in your body. It helps release tension and teaches you the contrast between tension and relaxation.
  - A quick way to do it:

        - Start at your feet – curl your toes and tense the muscles in your feet, hold for 5 seconds, then release and let them relax completely for 10 seconds. Notice the difference.
        - Then do the same for your calves (point toes up to tighten calves, hold, release), then thighs (tighten, hold, release).
        - Continue upward: buttocks, stomach, hands (make a fist), arms (bend elbow and tense bicep), shoulders (shrug up), neck (press head gently back), and face (scrunch up your face tight, then relax). Be careful with any injury areas.
        - After going through major muscle groups, you should feel a wave of relaxation.
    - This method can be done in about 10-15 minutes. It's excellent for winding down at night, or anytime you notice you're physically wound up. It's also a good distraction from anxious thoughts because you're focusing on your body.
- **Quick tension release:** If you don't have time for full PMR, you can do a short version: *inhale and squeeze all your muscles at once* (face, fists, core, legs) for a few seconds, then exhale and go limp. Do that a couple times. It can shake off a bit of the jitters.

These relaxation techniques, when practiced regularly, can reduce overall anxiety levels. In fact, many trauma survivors incorporate a daily breathing/relaxation routine (like 10 minutes in the morning and 10 at night). Over time, you may notice you feel a calmer baseline, and when stress spikes, you have a reliable method to bring it down.

Grounding Strategies

Grounding means pulling your mind out of the distressing memory or anxiety and anchoring it to the present, where you are safe. It's crucial during flashbacks, panic attacks, dissociative episodes, or even waves of grief. We already did one grounding exercise (5-4-3-2-1) in an earlier chapter. Here are some others:

- **The 5-4-3-2-1 Technique:** To recap, identify 5 things you see, 4 things you feel (tactile), 3 things you hear, 2 things you smell, 1 thing you taste. This engages all your senses and directs attention outward to your environment. It's like giving your mind a task that competes with the traumatic memory. It's simple but surprisingly effective. Keep it in your mental toolkit for moments when you feel "triggered" or detached.
- **Sensory Grounding Objects:** Many people carry a small object that can ground them. For example, a smooth stone, a stress ball, a fidget toy, or a vial of a scent like lavender oil. When panic or dissociation hits, you focus on the object: feel the texture of the stone, notice its color and temperature, or inhale the calming scent. The sensory input can break the loop of traumatic thought. Even running cold water over your hands or holding an ice cube can jolt you to the present if you're dissociating (the cold is very "here and now").

- **Describe Your Surroundings:** Wherever you are, start **narrating to yourself** (out loud if possible, or in your head) what you observe in neutral detail. E.g., "I am sitting at my desk. The table is brown wood. The window is open and I see the green tree outside. I hear cars passing. It is Tuesday, 3pm, and I am in my home, not in the past." This kind of factual description can ground you. You can also describe yourself to remind who/where you are: "My name is __. I am __ years old. I live in [city] in [year]. That bad thing happened long ago; it is not happening now. I am safe in this moment." This may feel silly but it reassures the disoriented brain of reality.

- **Grounding through Movement:** Doing something physical can also ground. For example, gently stomp your feet on the floor a few times (reminding yourself "these are my feet, here on the ground" — it connects you to the earth). Or press your palms together firmly and focus on that sensation. Some people do a few jumping jacks or push-ups – the feeling of muscles working and heart pumping can bring you out of your head.

The key with grounding is **finding what senses help you snap back**.

For some, sound is powerful (playing a strong beat of music or ringing a bell).

For others, touch (holding a textured item or a weighted blanket). Vision can be tricky if you're seeing flashbacks, but looking around intently for specific things (like "count all the blue items in the room") gives it a job.

Grounding is your go-to for those "emergency" moments of high distress or unreality. With practice, you'll get better at it, and perhaps need it less often as triggers lessen. But always keep some grounding trick in your back pocket.

Mindfulness and Meditation

Mindfulness is somewhat related to grounding but more of an ongoing practice. It means **paying attention to the present moment, on purpose, and non-judgmentally**. Meditation is one formal way to build mindfulness (like focusing on your breath), but you can also do everyday activities mindfully.

For trauma survivors, mindfulness helps in a few ways: it trains you to notice thoughts/feelings without immediately reacting. For instance, instead of being swept away by a wave of panic, you might learn to observe "there is a wave of panic in me" like watching an ocean wave rise and fall. This slight detachment can reduce suffering. Mindfulness also counteracts dissociation by gently anchoring you in now and in your body, in a tolerable way.

Some approachable mindfulness practices:

- **Basic Breath Meditation:** Sit comfortably. Close your eyes (or lower your gaze). Focus attention on your breathing – perhaps the feeling of air at your nostrils, or your belly rising/falling. When your mind wanders (which it will, a thousand times), gently bring it back to the breath without self-criticism. Start with just 5 minutes. It's okay if you feel restless or thoughts intrude; the practice is noticing and returning to the present. Over time, you can extend it. This trains concentration and calms the mind. It is best done early in the morning or late at night and a quiet environment is essential.
- **Body Scan:** This is a mindfulness exercise where you mentally scan your body from head to toe, paying attention to sensations without trying to change them. You might notice "tight jaw, tension in neck, warm hands, heart beating fast" – just notice. If any sensation is too upsetting, you can move past it. The body scan helps you get reacquainted with bodily feelings in a safe context, which is great if you tend to be disconnected. It can also cause you to release tension.
- **Mindful walking or eating:** Choose an everyday activity and do it mindfully. Say you pick walking. For 10 minutes, focus on the

experience of walking – how your feet feel hitting the ground, the swing of your arms, the air on your face, the sights and sounds around. If you catch your mind drifting into worries or memories, gently bring it back to the sensation of walking. Or eating: pick a meal or a small snack like a raisin. Eat slowly, noticing the textures, flavors, chewing motions, etc. Engaging fully in normal activities can ground and calm you, and bring a sense of simple pleasure that trauma often robs.

- **Mindfulness apps or classes:** If you find it hard to do on your own, consider guided meditations (there are many free apps and YouTube videos). Some meditations are specifically for trauma survivors (like focusing on safe places, or breathing for anxiety). Yoga classes (trauma-sensitive ones in particular) incorporate mindfulness too.

Research shows mindfulness can help reduce PTSD symptoms, particularly hyperarousal and avoidance. It should be noted that for some with severe trauma history, closing eyes and going inward can initially trigger flashbacks or emotions; if so, it's okay to start with very brief or external mindfulness (like focusing on sound or a visual focal point) and perhaps do it with support (like in a class). The goal is not to flood yourself but to gradually increase your window of tolerance for just being.

Self-Soothing and Sensory Comfort

Trauma survivors often have an elevated stress baseline, so it's crucial to deliberately engage in **self-soothing** – doing things that comfort and relax you. This overlaps with relaxation techniques, but extends to any healthy activity that gives you a sense of safety or pleasure.

Consider each of the 5 senses and think of a soothing input for each:

- **Vision:** Looking at something beautiful or calming. It could be nature (sitting in a park, watching clouds or water). Or a cozy room with low lighting. Some people find candles or soft string lights very soothing. Others might watch a favorite gentle movie or look through happy photos.
- **Sound:** Create a calming playlist of music that makes you feel safe or uplifted – could be soft instrumentals, nature sounds (rain, ocean), or songs with positive lyrics. Audio books or podcasts with friendly voices can also be comforting. Singing or humming to yourself can soothe (the vibrations actually calm the vagus nerve!).
- **Smell:** Certain scents can trigger calm. Lavender, chamomile, vanilla, or pine are commonly relaxing smells. You could use essential oils, incense, a scented candle, or even bake something that smells nice (like bread or cookies). The smell of a particular soap or lotion could bring comfort (some survivors like childlike scents like strawberry shampoo because it's innocent and positive).

- **Touch:** Tactile comfort is big. Wrapping yourself in a soft blanket, cuddling a pet or hugging a pillow/stuffed animal, taking a warm bath or shower (warmth is soothing and relaxes muscles), or having a weighted blanket (the gentle pressure can reduce anxiety). Some find brushing their hair or lotioning their skin slowly is calming (like giving care to your body). A stress ball to squeeze or clay to mold can release tension. If you have a partner or close friend, a safe hug or hand massage might help.

- **Taste:** While one must be cautious not to rely solely on food for comfort, a warm cup of herbal tea or hot cocoa can be very soothing – it's the warmth and the ritual. Some people find sucking on a peppermint or chewing gum helps ground them (strong flavors can snap you to present). Mindfully eating a small treat (like a piece of dark chocolate) savoring it fully can be a nice self-care moment. Just avoid anything that is itself triggering (some flavors or textures could remind you of unpleasant experiences – skip those).

Building a **"soothe box" or kit** is a great idea. This is a box or bag where you gather a few items that calm you: maybe a scented candle, a soft piece of fabric, a photo of a loved one or pet, an uplifting quote, your favorite tea packets, a stress ball, etc. When you're distressed, you can open your soothing box and use those items as a structured way to comfort yourself.

Another element of self-soothing is **inner self-talk**. Traumatic experiences can leave us with a harsh inner critic or a panicked inner child. Part of soothing is speaking to yourself kindly. For example, when anxious you might tell yourself, "It's understandable to feel this way. I am going to be okay. I'm taking steps to help myself. I am safe right now." It might feel forced at first, but imagine what a compassionate friend would say and try saying that to yourself. Over time, an internal compassionate voice can grow, which is immensely healing (and counters the negative messages trauma may have instilled).

Journaling and Expressive Writing

We did a journaling exercise earlier about emotions. Journaling in general is a well-established tool for coping. Writing about your thoughts and feelings can provide an outlet (especially if you have a lot you feel you can't say to others) and can bring clarity.

James Pennebaker's research on expressive writing found that people who wrote about traumatic experiences for 15-20 minutes a day over several days had improvements in health and mood (though it can be uncomfortable in the short term).

The idea is that writing helps you process and make sense of what happened, turning chaotic feelings into a coherent narrative.

Types of journaling to consider:

- **Free-writing "brain dump":** Just write whatever is on your mind, uncensored, for a set time (say 10 minutes). This is good when you feel overwhelmed and need to release. You might shred it or keep it; it doesn't matter, since it's for you.
- **Trauma narration:** Closer to therapy homework – writing the story of what happened, including how you felt then and now. Only do this in doses you can handle. Some find it empowering to see that they can write it and survive the memory, gradually reducing its power. But if it destabilizes you too much, it's okay to hold off or do it with guidance of a therapist. Even writing in third person ("She went through X…") can sometimes help to express it somewhat indirectly.
- **Gratitude or positive journaling:** Trauma skews towards negativity, so balancing it out intentionally can reshape your mindset. Each day or week, note a few things you're thankful for or small positive moments (a nice weather day, a friend's call, enjoying a meal). This doesn't erase problems, but over time it trains you to notice the good, which builds hope. Research suggests gratitude practices can improve mood and even physical health.

- **Future-self or letter writing:** Write a letter to your future self about what you hope for, or from your future self to current you giving encouragement. Or write a letter to someone (not to send) expressing things you need to say – maybe to the person who hurt you (to externalize anger or grief safely), or to someone who supported you (to reflect on gratitude).
- **Art journaling:** If writing isn't your thing, an alternative is drawing or collage. Sometimes drawing how you feel (even abstract scribbles or colors to represent emotions) can be another form of expression. Some people keep a sketchbook for this.
- **Bullet journal for triggers/symptoms:** A more analytical approach: track your symptoms and triggers in a log. For example, note each day if you had nightmares, and what you did before bed; or log when you felt anxious and see if you can link it to something. This data can help you and perhaps a therapist identify patterns and effective coping. For instance, you might realize, "Every time I watch the news at night, I get nightmares; maybe I should avoid news at night." Or "The week I exercised 3 times, I had fewer panic attacks."

Journaling provides a safe private space to articulate things. It can also show progress – reading entries from months ago might reveal how far you've come (or help you catch if you're sliding back so you can adjust). And as mentioned earlier, there is evidence that writing helps reduce stress and improve immune function – likely because it reduces internal rumination; once it's on paper, your brain might let it rest a bit.

One caution: If you find journaling about trauma leaves you more upset and you have trouble calming down after, make sure to use coping skills post-writing.

Maybe do a free-write about trauma for 10 minutes, then immediately do a grounding exercise or watch a funny video to re-center. Or save heavy topics for therapy sessions where you have support.

Lifestyle and Routine

While coping skills above address immediate symptoms, we mustn't forget basic **lifestyle habits** that form the foundation of mental health:

- **Sleep:** Aim for a regular sleep schedule and sufficient hours (7-9 for adults typically). We know PTSD often brings nightmares and insomnia. Using relaxation techniques at bedtime, keeping a cool dark room, avoiding screens an hour before bed, and perhaps using comfort objects (like a weighted blanket or soft music) can help. If nightmares are a major issue, some find success with a technique called Imagery Rehearsal Therapy (essentially rewriting your nightmares' storyline when awake to be less frightening – a therapist can guide this).
  Additionally, if you wake from a nightmare, have a plan: do a grounding exercise, remind yourself where you are, maybe read something calming or have a ritual like making herbal tea. Consistent wake-up and bedtimes help regulate your body clock, which can ease sleep trouble over time. If nothing helps, consult a doctor; short-term sleep medication or specific therapies might be needed.
- **Exercise:** Regular physical activity is one of the best trauma-busters. It releases endorphins, reduces stress hormones, improves mood, and can even improve sleep and concentration. Cardiovascular exercises like running, walking, swimming, or cycling are great to burn off anxiety. Weight training or yoga can build confidence and body connection. Choose something you enjoy (or least dislike!). Even a **20-minute brisk walk** a few times a week can make a difference. Group classes (if you're comfortable) could add a social element which is also healing. Listen to your body; don't push too hard if you're feeling particularly dissociative or triggered by exercise (sometimes elevated heart rate can remind of panic). Start slow. Overtime, many survivors credit exercise as a key part of recovery – it was their safe way to release emotions and feel strong. It literally can grow new brain cells in areas like the hippocampus, which trauma can shrink.

- **Nutrition:** Eating a balanced, regular diet supports your body's healing. Trauma often throws off appetite; some overeat for comfort, others undereat due to stress. Try not to skip meals – low blood sugar can worsen anxiety or irritability. Emphasize protein, whole grains, fruits, and veggies to keep your energy stable. Omega-3 rich foods (like fish, walnuts, flaxseed) are thought to help brain health. Limit caffeine if you're anxious (maybe switch that afternoon coffee to herbal tea). Limit alcohol – while it might numb feelings short-term, it disrupts sleep and exacerbates mood issues long-term (and can lead to dependency). The goal is to nourish yourself – which is a form of self-care and body respect that trauma might have taken away. If cooking is daunting, consider simple meals or healthy prepared options. Hydration matters too (dehydration can mimic anxiety symptoms).

- **Structure and Routine:** Trauma can make life feel chaotic or out of control. Establishing a gentle routine can restore a sense of predictability and safety. This could be as simple as having a morning ritual (wake up, stretch, eat breakfast, get dressed at around the same time each day) or a nighttime wind-down routine. If you're not working, plan small activities in the day (like a walk at 4pm, TV show at 7pm, journal at 8pm). Routines provide a scaffold for recovery – you know what comes next, which leaves less room for ruminating. But also keep it flexible; don't beat yourself up if you deviate. The idea is routine as a friend, not a rigid rule.
- **Social Connection:** Isolation is the enemy to recovery. Humans heal in community. While trauma (especially interpersonal trauma) can make trust hard, gradual reconnection is healing. This might mean confiding in one friend or family member about what you're going through. Or joining a support group for trauma survivors (in person or online) to share and hear "Me too" from others. Even casual social interactions help – chatting with a coworker, attending a faith group or hobby club, volunteering. Being around people (safe people) reminds you that you're not alone and provides potential joy, distraction, and support. If crowds are hard, start small – maybe one-on-one meetings in calm environments. Over time, aim not to let the

trauma cage you away from relationships. Good connections literally release oxytocin, an antidote to stress chemistry.

- **Avoidance vs. Engagement:** A tricky balance – we know avoiding triggers maintains PTSD, but also diving into overwhelming situations too fast can backfire.

Coping means knowing when to gently push yourself to face things and when to step back and rest. As you practice tools, you might become braver – perhaps you'll gradually drive again after a car accident by going one block further each day.

Or if sexual intimacy is difficult after an assault, you might work with a therapist and a patient partner to slowly regain comfort (lots of communication and stepwise exposure to touch).

The coping tools you learn (breathing, grounding, thought reframing) will support you when you choose to engage with triggers gradually. It's like building muscle – little challenges will strengthen you, and you retreat when needed to recover.

Eventually, avoidance shrinks and your life grows.

A note on **faith and spirituality as coping** (especially given our holistic approach including Islamic insights):

Many trauma survivors find solace in prayer, reading scripture, or participating in religious community.

For some, faith provides a framework that suffering has meaning or that a higher power is supporting them.

If you are religious or spiritual, lean into those practices that give you comfort – whether it's praying five times a day, meditating, or talking to a faith leader.

Just be cautious if any religious thoughts are actually harming your self-view (e.g., "this trauma was a punishment from God" – that kind of belief can impede healing).

Often, consulting a compassionate faith mentor can help reframe it (perhaps viewing it instead as a test of patience or an opportunity for growth, as per one’s beliefs).

Creating a Safe Space

It's important to **have a place and time where you feel safe** to relax. If your home is your sanctuary, make a corner of it especially cozy for destressing – maybe your bedroom or a chair with a soft blanket and your grounding objects. If home is stressful (say you live with many people or in a noisy area), identify another safe spot – perhaps a library, a specific park bench in daylight, a room in a friend's house. Use that space intentionally for calming down if needed.

Also, schedule "**worry time**" if racing thoughts bother you constantly. This is a cognitive trick: set aside 15 minutes a day where you allow yourself to worry and think about whatever (maybe write it out).

The rest of the day, when worries intrude, tell yourself "Not now, I'll think about that at 6:00 during my worry time." It sounds odd, but it can contain the constant anxiety to a smaller window and give you more mental peace otherwise.

Lastly, **patience** and **celebrating small wins** are vital coping attitudes. Healing is gradual; notice and praise yourself for each step ("I had only one panic attack this week vs two last week, progress!" or "I slept 5 hours straight, yay!").

When setbacks occur, don't view them as failure – they're a normal part of the process. Use them to learn (maybe you got overwhelmed because you skipped self-care, so next time you'll try not to).

To avoid burnout in recovery: alternate challenging yourself with nurturing yourself. For example, if you had a hard therapy session (challenge), that evening do something soothing or fun (nurture) as balance.

Over time, your capacity for dealing with stress will increase, but it's always good to be kind to yourself.

You now have quite the toolkit: breathing, grounding, mindfulness, journaling, social support, physical care, and more. It's a lot, but you don't have to implement everything at once. Maybe pick one or two things to focus on this week (say, deep breathing every morning and going for a walk on Monday, Wednesday, Friday). Add gradually. Think of these as lifelong resilience skills – beneficial not only for trauma but for life's future stresses too.

Next chapters will delve into some special topics: cultural aspects of trauma, intergenerational effects, and community healing – because trauma and healing don't happen in a vacuum of just the individual. And we'll have a section for those in helper roles, like trainee therapists, on how to care for others without burning out themselves.

CHAPTER 10: CULTURAL SENSITIVITY AND STIGMA IN TRAUMA RECOVERY

Trauma doesn't happen in isolation – it's experienced and interpreted through the lens of one's **culture, community, and society**.

In this chapter, we'll explore how culture can impact a survivor's response to trauma and access to healing. We'll also tackle the issue of **stigma**: unfortunately, mental health struggles like PTSD are often misunderstood or stigmatized in many societies. Fear of judgment can make people hide their pain or avoid seeking help. By understanding these cultural and social factors, we can better support ourselves and others on the healing journey.

The Role of Culture in Trauma

Culture shapes our beliefs, values, and even how we express distress. What might be considered a **"normal" trauma reaction** in one culture could be viewed differently in another. For example, in some cultures open emotional expression (crying, screaming) after trauma is accepted or even encouraged (like wailing at funerals in some traditions).

In others, stoicism and keeping feelings private is valued. Neither is right or wrong, but it affects how a survivor may behave and what they feel is "okay" to show.

Cultural Concepts of Distress: Different cultures have unique ways of describing and handling suffering. In some communities, trauma might be described in physical terms more than emotional ones (like "my heart is hurting" or specific syndromes).

For instance, some Latinx cultures talk about "susto" (a fright illness where a part of the soul is thought to leave the body after a traumatic scare).

In East Asian contexts, you might see trauma manifest as somatic complaints like headaches or fatigue because of norms around discussing mental health. Indigenous cultures might interpret trauma through a spiritual lens – perhaps as disharmony that needs ritual healing.

It's important to understand these perspectives, especially if you're seeking help: a therapist aware of your cultural background will honor these expressions and incorporate that understanding.

Historical and Collective Trauma: Some cultures carry what's known as historical trauma – collective trauma experienced by a group across generations (like slavery, colonization, war, genocide). This can influence a survivor's experience.

For example, an African American person might carry not only personal trauma but also the stress of systemic racism and the historical trauma of their ancestors. This might make them wary of predominantly white medical systems, or their trauma triggers might include racialized elements.

Recognizing historical trauma is crucial; healing often needs to include community and cultural reclamation (like connecting with traditions, language, or historical knowledge to find strength and identity beyond the trauma).

Another example: Many Native American communities approach trauma healing with community and spirituality – e.g., talking circles, sweat lodge ceremonies, story-telling, connecting to land – as a way to mend not just the individual but the community web that was torn by past colonization and forced assimilation.

These practices might not be found in a mainstream therapy manual but are profoundly therapeutic for those communities.

Gender and Cultural Norms: Culture intersects with gender roles in trauma response. In some cultures, men are expected to be "strong" and not show vulnerability, which can make it extremely hard for male survivors to admit fear or seek help – they may channel it into anger or substance use instead.

Women in certain traditional cultures might fear that admitting sexual assault, for instance, could bring shame or even danger (like "honor" violence or being ostracized). LGBTQ+ individuals might have trauma compounded by cultural stigma against their identity, and may not find culturally competent support readily.

Understanding one's cultural context can actually provide **resources** too.

Each culture has coping traditions – be it through faith, family kinship, music and dance, or connection to nature. Embracing positive cultural practices can be healing.

For example, a Muslim survivor might find comfort in daily prayers or specific supplications (like dua's for ease in hardship), or reading the story of Prophet Ayyub (A.S.) who endured great trials.

Or a Japanese survivor might find calm in the tea ceremony or martial arts philosophy. Or a Black American might draw resilience from the legacy of Black survival and the community strength seen in church gatherings or art.

Everyone's different, but tapping into cultural strengths is powerful. Therapists call this being "culturally responsive" – using the client's cultural background as a source of resilience, not an obstacle.

Language barriers: If your first language isn't English (or the main language of where you live), it can be hard to express deep emotions in a second language. Emotions are strongly tied to language nuances. In therapy, if possible, find a provider who speaks your language or use an interpreter – trauma therapy through interpreters can work, though it adds complexity.

Even journaling or speaking to supportive folks in your native language can help process things more fully. There are concepts (like certain types of grief or cultural idioms) that just don't translate neatly; you shouldn't have to abandon your cultural lens to heal.

Stigma and Seeking Help

Stigma is a huge barrier. Many people fear being seen as "crazy" or weak if they admit to mental health issues. This is amplified in communities where mental illness is not well-understood or is taboo.

For instance, some Asian cultures emphasize saving face – one might worry that seeing a therapist will shame their family or that others will treat them differently.

In certain macho environments (military, perhaps), PTSD might historically have been seen as a lack of toughness (though this is changing thankfully).

Consequences of stigma: It leads to avoidance or delay of treatment. People suffer in silence, maybe self-medicating with alcohol or drugs.

They might feel isolated thinking "it's just me, I'm broken." The truth is PTSD is a medical condition, not a moral failing. Just like you wouldn't shame someone for having a broken leg, mental trauma isn't something to shame.

Part of recovery often involves actively challenging the stigma you may have internalized. For example, telling yourself: "Seeking help is a form of strength, not weakness. I am taking responsibility for my health." Or educating family members: "PTSD is a real condition that can happen to anyone after severe stress – it doesn't mean I'm unstable or dangerous, it means I'm injured and need help to heal."

In some communities, mental health issues are attributed to spiritual causes (like possession, curses, or as punishment).

This can either add stigma ("you must've done wrong to be punished") or simply misdirect from medical solutions.

It might be beneficial to explore both avenues in such cases – e.g., if a family believes in spiritual affliction, working with a faith healer and a therapist might be a culturally sensitive compromise.

The key is not to ignore the psychological aspects while respecting spiritual beliefs.

How to combat stigma:

- **Education:** Many just don't understand PTSD. Sharing information (pamphlets, websites, maybe having a community workshop or talk by a professional) can demystify it. Learning that PTSD has biological bases (like changes in the brain) and effective treatments can shift perspectives from "just get over it" to "oh, this is a health issue to address."
- **Storytelling:** When individuals share their own experiences of mental health (like public figures or peers in a group), it breaks the "I'm the only one" feeling. Hearing someone say "I had panic attacks and got help and now I'm doing better" can inspire others to not be ashamed. Support groups, as mentioned, are great for this – seeing others who validate your experience reduces self-stigma.
- **Language:** Even the language we use can reduce stigma. For example, saying "I have PTSD" or "I am healing from trauma" rather than derogatory phrases like "I'm messed up" or someone else saying "she's gone nuts." Using respectful, medical terminology frames it correctly. Also, reminding people that PTSD is common (millions have it) normalizes seeking help.
- **Privacy and choice:** Some fear stigma so much that they won't seek help publicly. Thankfully there are more anonymous resources now (helplines, online therapy, etc.). While ideally we want a world where no one fears being seen at a therapist, in the meantime, know that you can access help in discreet ways if needed. What matters is you get support.
- **Find allies:** Maybe there's one person in your family or friend circle who "gets it" or is at least open-minded. Enlist their aid. For example, bring them to a family therapy session to help advocate for you, or have them help explain to your parents what you're going through. Sometimes a respected community member (like a pastor or elder) can influence others to be more understanding if they stand by you or speak about trauma as something requiring care.

Important: You are not weak for being affected by trauma. In fact, surviving it, even with scars, is a sign of strength. If anyone around you implies "just toughen up" or "why aren't you over it?", that is ignorance speaking. Try to educate them; if they refuse to understand, seek support elsewhere. Sometimes families or cultures are not supportive initially – in such cases, build your own support network (friends, support group, therapist) who validate you. Later, those skeptical family members may come around when they see your improvement or learn more.

Cultural sensitivity also applies to therapists. If you feel a therapist doesn't understand your cultural background or dismisses something important to you (like spiritual beliefs or family customs), it's okay to bring that up or even find a different therapist.

The therapeutic relationship should feel safe for all of you – including your cultural identity. More therapists these days are trained in multicultural competency, but some may still impose their own worldview inadvertently.

Speak up: e.g., "*In my culture, talking to strangers about family issues is frowned upon. It's hard for me to open up because of that.*" A good therapist will navigate that with you, not push you or judge your family.

Community Healing: On a larger scale, communities are recognizing trauma's impact and creating local healing initiatives. For instance, some neighborhoods form trauma-informed community programs (like peer-run wellness centers). Ethnic communities might integrate cultural rituals into mental health care (like drumming circles for African diaspora trauma healing, or community feasts where elders share resilience stories).

Being involved in such communal processes can heal not just individuals but relationships and collective spirit.

To summarize, **culture can be a source of both challenge and strength** in trauma recovery. Awareness of cultural and societal influences helps tailor healing to be most effective for you. Reducing stigma is a collective effort – each time you bravely reach out, or gently correct a misconception, you're contributing to a more trauma-informed society.

Faith-Based Insight: Finding Strength in Community and Faith

In many faith traditions, enduring hardship is not only a personal trial but a collective one – communities of faith often rally around those in distress.

For example, in Islam, there is an emphasis on ummah (community) and shura (consultation/support): leaning on fellow believers and scholars for comfort and guidance can be a form of healing.

The Prophet Muhammad (peace be upon him) said, "The believers, in their mutual kindness, compassion and sympathy, are just like one body. When one of the limbs suffers, the whole body responds to it with wakefulness and fever." (Sahih Muslim: 2586)

This saying reminds trauma survivors that they are not meant to suffer alone – their pain is our pain, and shared compassion is part of the remedy.

If you belong to a faith community, consider confiding in a trusted faith leader or support group within it. For instance, some churches have Stephen Ministries or pastoral counseling; mosques might have support circles or knowledgeable counselors.

Integrating spiritual counsel with psychological help can address the soul-level questions trauma raises ("***Why did God allow this? How can I trust again?***").

A wise mentor might point you to narratives of perseverance in scripture – like Prophet Ayyub's steadfastness through illness and loss, or Prophet Yusuf's (Joseph's) journey from trauma (being betrayed and imprisoned) to forgiveness and flourishing – showing that suffering can lead to wisdom and greater good in time.

Also, engaging in communal acts of worship can soothe: the rhythmic recitation of holy texts, congregational prayers, singing hymns – these can regulate breathing, foster unity, and give a sense of something larger holding you.

In one study on trauma survivors, those who engaged in spiritual practices reported a sense of peace and meaning even amidst pain.

Prayer, meditation, or reading spiritual texts when done mindfully can be akin to a therapeutic session with the Divine – a safe space to pour out your heart and seek solace.

However, be cautious of any religious framing that increases guilt or stigma.

If someone says "*your faith must be weak if you're anxious*" or "*just pray more and it'll go away,*" remember that mental health struggles are not a sign of weak faith – prophets themselves wept and felt fear.

The Quran itself acknowledges human grief and anxiety (even Mary (Bibi Maryam, mother of Prophet Isa (A.S), a righteous figure, said *she wished she were dead from her labor pains – a raw expression of distress*, **Quran 19:23**, yet she was not condemned for it).

So your emotional reactions do not make you a bad believer; they make you human.

Use faith as a **support**, not a cudgel to beat yourself up with.

At the same time, faith can motivate healing. Believing that "***Allah does not burden a soul beyond what it can bear" (Quran 2:286***) might instill hope that you have, or will be given, the strength to overcome this – not alone, but with God's help and community's help.

Many survivors find purpose in turning their trauma into service – like volunteering, helping others in similar situations, or advocacy – which aligns with values of compassion and can transform pain into something meaningful.

In essence, draw on your **cultural and spiritual resources** as a complement to therapy: let your community hold you, let your faith uplift you, and let stigma fall away in the face of truth and empathy.

Healing is your birthright across all languages and creeds; seek it without shame.

As a community, when we recognize trauma as a wound to be healed collectively, we live out that ideal of being like one body, supporting each part in pain.

In the next chapter, we will discuss trauma beyond the individual – how it can echo through generations and how whole communities can approach healing together. Then, a chapter for those in helping roles to guard their own wellbeing.

We're building towards a comprehensive understanding that trauma healing is not just personal, but can be familial and societal as well.

CHAPTER 11: INTERGENERATIONAL TRAUMA – HEALING ACROSS GENERATIONS

Trauma has a ripple effect that can extend beyond the person who directly experienced it.

Intergenerational trauma (also called transgenerational or multigenerational trauma) refers to the ways trauma can be passed down from one generation to the next. This can happen through direct relationships (parents to children) or even at a community level (a whole group carrying trauma from historical events).

In this chapter, we'll explore how trauma can echo through families in terms of behaviors, beliefs, and even biology.

More importantly, we'll discuss how to break the cycle – how families and communities can foster resilience and healing that stops trauma from transmitting further.

How Trauma Transfers Between Generations

It might sound strange – how can you be affected by something that happened to your ancestors or parents before you were even born? But research and anecdotal evidence show this is a real phenomenon. Here are some ways it happens:

- **Family Environment and Parenting:** Parents who have unresolved trauma may inadvertently project their fears or patterns onto their children.
    - For example, a mother who was abused might be overly anxious and protective, or have difficulty with emotional closeness, thus the child grows up under constant fear or emotional distance.
    - Or a father with PTSD from war might have anger outbursts or emotional numbing that the children witness and adapt to (walking on eggshells, etc.).
    - Children internalize these behaviors or are affected by chaotic or withdrawn caregiving. Sometimes, traumatized parents may even reenact or continue cycles of abuse if they haven't healed – the classic case of "the abused becomes the abuser" in some instances, though many break that pattern.
- **Unspoken Stories and Emotions:** Some families never talk about a traumatic past event (like a genocide, migration trauma, etc.). Yet, the emotional undertone of grief or fear might permeate the household. Kids pick up on that unspoken stress. They may not know the story, but they experience its effects – perhaps through overprotective rules, or certain triggers that make the parent react strongly (like the sound of sirens making a refugee parent panic). The child might develop anxiety or behaviors around those triggers too, without fully understanding why.
- **Beliefs and Worldview:** Traumatized communities may develop shared beliefs like "the world isn't safe" or "we don't trust outsiders." They then raise children with those beliefs.

    - For instance, Indigenous communities traumatized by colonization might pass on a wariness of government institutions to their kids, which could manifest as reluctance to engage with healthcare or education systems (due to historical harm).
    - African American families might teach their children very vigilant strategies for dealing with police or racism – a necessary adaptation, but one rooted in collective trauma, which also means the child grows up in a state of vigilance. The beliefs help survival but can also carry psychological strain.
- **Epigenetics:** Fascinating new research suggests trauma can leave biological imprints on how genes function, which can be passed to offspring. These aren't changes in the gene code itself, but in gene expression – called epigenetic changes.
    - For example, children or grandchildren of Holocaust survivors have been found to have differences in stress hormone regulation compared to the general population.
    - A recent study on descendants of survivors of war in Syria indicated altered patterns in certain genes related to stress response.
    - In rats, it's been shown that if a parent rat is exposed to a certain trauma or even a smell paired with shock, the offspring show heightened stress responses to that smell – even if they never experienced the shock themselves.
    - This suggests some heritable adaptation: basically, the parent's trauma "preps" the next generation's biology to be on alert for similar dangers. It's like a head start on survival, but in a safer environment it may manifest as anxiety or other issues. These findings, while still being understood, provide a scientific underpinning to the intuition communities have had: that the pain of one generation can indeed live in the bodies of the next.

Knowing trauma can pass down is not to blame our ancestors or parents, but to understand our context. It can be liberating – like, if you suffer from depression or hypervigilance and then learn "Oh, my grandmother lived through a war and never dealt with it, and that vibe sort of came through the family," it might reframe your struggle not as purely your fault but as part of a larger legacy that you can now address.

Breaking the Cycle

The great news is that intergenerational trauma does not have to continue indefinitely. **Healing can also be passed down**. When one person in a family heals (even partly), they often become a "cycle breaker", changing the narrative for those after them. Here are ways to break free:

- **Acknowledge and Talk About It:** Bringing secrets or unspoken pain into the open is a powerful first step. Family therapy or just honest conversations in a family can start the healing.
  For instance, if a parent who lost their sibling in a violent event never spoke of it and was always just "angry," telling that story to their now-adult child might foster understanding on both sides.
  The child realizes "Dad wasn't angry at me; he was hurting from loss," and the dad might finally process some grief by sharing it. If older generations are alive, approach them gently: they may initially resist ("that's the past, I don't want to relive it"), but perhaps framing it as wanting to learn from their experiences or honor them can help. Even if they don't open up, you can do your own research on your family history or cultural history and then discuss patterns with a counselor.
- **Rituals of Healing:** Many cultures have rituals to heal past trauma or honor ancestors. Participating in these can be symbolic closures.
  - For example, some Indigenous communities hold intergenerational healing circles where elders share traumas and younger folks share their impact, concluding with rituals to release that pain collectively.
  - In Rwandan communities post-genocide, commemoration ceremonies combined with discussions aim to prevent transmission of hate or fear to youth.
  - As an individual, you might create a personal ritual: writing a letter to an ancestor forgiving them for passing on their trauma, or visiting a significant site and saying a prayer for peace. Ritual engages the heart and spirit, which is important beyond intellectual understanding.

- **Parenting with Awareness:** If you have children (or plan to), being mindful of how your trauma could affect your parenting is key. This doesn't mean you have to be perfect (no parent is), but you can make conscious efforts to break patterns.
    - For instance, if you grew up in an abusive home, you might attend parenting classes to learn non-violent discipline, or go to therapy to ensure you won't repeat emotional neglect. It also means when you slip up (maybe you yell and it echoes how your dad yelled at you), you acknowledge it, apologize to your child, and explain at an age-appropriate level, maybe tying it to why you're working on it ("I'm sorry I yelled. It's something I'm trying to do less because I know it hurts. My dad used to yell at me a lot and I'm working so our family is different."
    - This could be a powerful narrative for change, showing children that improvement is possible). Being a cycle-breaking parent often involves inner child work: healing the part of you that was a child, giving yourself the care you didn't get so you can give it to your kids. It can be deeply rewarding – many trauma survivors say raising their children in a healthier environment was healing for them too, as it "rewrote" their own childhood in a way.
- **Therapy and Support for Next Generations:** If you recognize signs of anxiety or trauma in your kids that likely stem from your experiences (or their own, if they went through something like witnessing your PTSD episodes or a community trauma), don't hesitate to involve them in counseling too. Family therapy can address dynamic issues.
    - For example, a veteran with PTSD might do a few family sessions so the spouse and kids understand triggers and how to cope together, thus reducing everyone's stress. There are trauma-informed programs specifically for families. Breaking the cycle is often a group project!
- **Epigenetic Hope:** On the biology front, epigenetic changes are not necessarily permanent; environment and behaviors can potentially reverse or mitigate them. A nurturing, low-stress upbringing can potentially dial back the stress hyper-reactivity that might've been

passed down. Essentially, by giving the next generation lots of safety and support, you may help their genes express themselves in a healthier way. It's poetic: love and care might be as biologically powerful as trauma, in the opposite direction.

- **Strengths of Ancestors:** Sometimes what's passed down isn't just trauma but also incredible resilience, wisdom, and culture. Leaning into those strengths can break the negative part of the cycle. For example, if you come from a line of survivors (Holocaust survivors, refugees, etc.), you likely inherited some survivor resilience too – perhaps determination, creative problem-solving, faith, humor as coping, strong family loyalty. Recognize and celebrate those traits in yourself and teach them to your kids. That way the narrative becomes, "Our ancestors went through terrible things, but they endured and we carry their strength; we honor them by living fully and not letting the trauma define us."

Community Healing from Historical Trauma

When trauma is collective (like war, colonization, racial oppression), healing often needs collective efforts:

- **Education and Acknowledgment:** Communities benefit from official acknowledgments of historical trauma (think truth and reconciliation commissions, memorials, apologies from governments). That validation can trickle down to the individual psyche: "Our pain is seen." It might not solve everything, but it opens a door.
- **Reviving Culture:** For colonized or oppressed groups, reclaiming language, traditions, and spirituality that were suppressed can restore pride and identity, which buffers against trauma's effects. E.g., Aboriginal healing camps that teach youth their language and ceremonies have noted improvements in those youths' mental health and break substance abuse patterns.
- **Collective Projects:** Engaging in activism or community projects to rectify or address the source of trauma can be empowering. For descendants of trauma, fighting for social justice or volunteering in community service can transform helplessness into purposeful action. It also forges bonds with others who "get it," replacing isolation with solidarity.

In essence, to break intergenerational trauma, we do the opposite of what trauma does. Trauma often silences – so we encourage open dialogue.

Trauma isolates – so we connect. Trauma breeds mistrust – so we cultivate trust and safety.

Trauma shames – so we honor and empower.

By doing so at personal, family, and community levels, we can send forward a legacy not of pain, but of resilience and growth.

It's not easy, and it won't erase what happened to past generations. But it can mean that the trauma stops with you, and future generations inherit less of that burden. As one famous saying (attributed to a child Holocaust survivor) goes, "Trauma decontextualized in a person over time can look like personality. Trauma decontextualized in a family over time can look like family traits. Trauma decontextualized in people over time can look like culture."

By recontextualizing and healing it, we can reclaim identity separate from trauma.

You might be reading this as a cycle-breaker in your family or community. It's a brave role. Remember to also break the cycle of trauma self-care: meaning, where your ancestors had to just "push through" without help, you are allowed to seek help and care for yourself.

You doing therapy or practicing coping or asking for support is not a weakness, it's a revolutionary act they may not have been able to do. In that sense, your healing honors them by not letting what hurt them destroy you too.

Finally, our next chapter is geared towards those who support trauma survivors – therapists in training or anyone in a caregiver role – on how to hold space and protect themselves from secondary trauma or burnout.

They are humans, too.

If you're not in that category, you might still find useful insights into what good support looks like and why boundaries for helpers are important. Then we'll conclude our journey.

CHAPTER 12: FOR THERAPISTS-IN-TRAINING AND CAREGIVERS – SUPPORTING OTHERS WITHOUT BURNING OUT

Throughout this book, we've focused on the survivor's perspective. But what about those who are helping trauma survivors?

Whether you're a therapist (or training to be one), a counselor, a support group leader, or even just a supportive friend/family member, supporting someone through trauma can be both rewarding and challenging.

There's the delicate art of **holding safe space** – creating an environment where the survivor feels heard, validated, and not judged.

There's also the risk of **vicarious trauma or burnout** for the helper – hearing trauma stories or constantly caring for others' pain can start to weigh on you mentally and emotionally.

In this chapter, we'll give guidance for helpers on how to be there for survivors in a healthy, effective way, while also taking care of themselves.

After all, you can not pour from an empty cup.

Holding Safe Space

To "hold space" means to be fully present with someone, offering them a container of empathy and acceptance in which they can express themselves.

Here's how to do that:

- **Empathy and Active Listening:** This is the cornerstone. Listen to the survivor's words and their feelings.
  - Show that you're engaged: maintain appropriate eye contact, nod, use verbal encouragers ("I see," "That sounds really hard," etc.).
  - Reflect back what you hear: "It sounds like you felt really betrayed when that happened."
  - Validate their emotions ("Anyone would be angry in that situation; it makes sense you feel that way").
  - Even if their experiences or reactions seem foreign to you, try to put yourself in their shoes.
  - Avoid jumping to give advice or fixing – initially, just witness their story with compassion.
  - Sometimes just saying, "I'm so sorry that happened to you. I'm here with you," can be incredibly powerful.
- **Non-Judgment and Patience:** Trauma can make people act in ways that might seem irrational or frustrating from the outside (like lashing out, or staying in unhealthy situations).
  - As a supporter, suspend judgment.
  - Understand these are coping strategies or trauma reactions, not character flaws.
  - Be patient with their pace of healing.
  - Don't say things like "You should be over it by now" or "Why didn't you do X then?" – these questions can come off as blaming.
  - Instead, focus on what they need now.
  - Similarly, respect their decisions: if they're not ready to confront something or to seek professional help, you can gently encourage but not force.

    - People heal on their own timeline.
- **Creating Safety:** If you're a professional, this may mean literal confidentiality (ensuring what is said is private) and also reliability (keeping your appointments, being on time, maintaining a calm environment).
    - If you're a friend, it might mean meeting in a place they feel comfortable, or taking steps like silencing your phone so there are no disruptions.
    - Safety also comes from consistency – being that steady presence they can rely on.
    - As a ***therapist-in-training***, learn about trauma-informed care principles as we covered – apply them.
        - For instance, give the survivor as much choice and control in the session as possible ("We can talk about whatever you feel is most pressing today" or "If you want to pause or take a break, just let me know"). Choice counters the helplessness of trauma.
- **Boundaries with Compassion:** Holding space doesn't mean letting the person do anything without any limits – boundaries are actually part of safety.
    - For professionals, ethical boundaries are clear (e.g., you're not their friend, you're their therapist – you provide structured support).
    - For personal relationships, boundaries mean taking care not to let attempts to help slide into unhealthy enabling or blurring of roles.
        - For example, if your adult sibling is trauma-affected and copes by drinking and calling you in the middle of the night everyday extremely intoxicated, holding space might mean saying, "*I love you and I want to support you. I will talk to you and help you find resources, but I can't do that at 2am when you've been drinking, because that's not healthy for either of us. Let's talk when you're sober tomorrow.*" It's a gentle boundary: you still care, but you're guiding them toward healthier interaction.

    - In therapy, boundaries include time management (start and end sessions on time), not sharing too much of your personal life, etc.
    - It might feel "less warm" to enforce boundaries, but boundaries actually make the survivor feel safe in the long run (they know what to expect, they know the relationship is stable and not overly entangled).

- **Normalize and Educate (when appropriate):** Part of holding space can include gently educating the survivor about trauma and common responses, so they feel less alone or crazy.
    - For instance, if someone says, "I'm going mad; I can't even remember parts of the trauma," you, as a therapist, can explain dissociative amnesia is a known phenomenon and is the brain's way of protecting, etc.
    - If you're a friend with some knowledge, you might say, "*Actually that sounds like a very common trauma response I read about – it's not just you.*" Careful though: don't turn the conversation into a lecture.
    - Use education as a tool for empowerment, not to take the focus off their feelings. And tailor it to what they want to know; some survivors are curious about the science, others just want emotional support.

- **Collaboration:** If you're a therapist, make therapy a collaboration. Set goals together. Check in often: "*How is this approach working for you? Does anything we're doing in session feel unhelpful or too much?*".
    - For supporters, collaborate in problem-solving: "What do you feel would help you most right now? We can brainstorm together." Emphasize their voice and choices. That fosters empowerment – which is exactly what trauma robs.
- **Cultural Sensitivity:** As we elaborated in the previous chapter, be mindful of the person's cultural background and personal values. If you don't know, ask respectfully.

E.g., “Is there anything about your background or beliefs that you think would be important for me to know so I can support you best?”

- **For professionals**, incorporate their cultural healing practices if possible (maybe they find prayer helpful – you could integrate a moment of silence or prayer if they wish; or if they use certain cultural metaphors, use that language).

If you are not familiar with their background, do a bit of your own research or consultation to avoid missteps.

For friends, just avoid making assumptions – e.g., don’t say “I know how you feel” if you clearly have a different life context; better to say “I can’t imagine exactly what you’re going through, but I want to understand and I’m here for you.”

Self-Care for the Helper (Avoiding Burnout and Secondary Trauma)

Hearing trauma stories or being around someone in intense pain can start to weigh on the helper over time. **Secondary traumatic stress** (also called compassion fatigue or vicarious trauma) is when you, the helper, begin to experience trauma-like symptoms from exposure to others' trauma.

You might have nightmares about their stories, become extra anxious or hypervigilant, or start feeling helpless or numb in general.

Burnout is a more general exhaustion (emotional and physical) from overwork or extreme stress in caring for others, leading to decreased capacity or cynicism. Helpers are at risk for both, especially if they neglect their own needs.

To prevent or mitigate this:

- **Set Realistic Limits:** You cannot save or fix anyone. Even as a therapist, you are a facilitator, not a savior. Recognize that you provide tools and support, but the survivor must do their own healing work too. This mindset helps reduce feelings of personal failure if someone isn't improving quickly.
    - For personal supporters: limit the time and energy you give in a sustainable way. E.g., maybe you tell your friend you can meet for coffee once a week to talk and check-in, but you can't be on call every day. Or if you're caring for a traumatized spouse at home, ensure you have an hour to yourself each day or a day off weekly where someone else can be with them. It's not selfish; it's necessary to recharge.
    - If you're a trainee therapist, don't overload your caseload with exclusively heavy trauma cases if possible; mix it up if you can or at least space them out in the week, and use supervision to vent and process your feelings (supervision is a MUST – talk about those cases with a mentor, it offloads some of the weight).

- **Self-Awareness and Reflection:** Pay attention to your own emotional state. Signs of secondary trauma/burnout include: feeling emotionally exhausted, irritable, or numb; dreading your sessions or interactions; intrusive imagery or constant worry about the person; difficulty sleeping; cynicism or hopelessness about trauma in general; even physical symptoms like headaches or fatigue. If you notice these, it's time to up your self-care and possibly seek support for yourself (therapists often benefit from their own therapy; friends may talk to other friends or a counselor about the stress of supporting someone).
  - Don't brush it off – catching it early can prevent a full burnout. Journaling about your experiences can help you separate what's yours and what's not (for instance, you might journal: "*I felt a tightness in my chest when I heard their story of abandonment – could it be reminding me of something in me*? Or am I just feeling deep empathy pain?" That awareness helps to not carry it unconsciously).
- **Debrief and Seek Peer Support:** If you're in a helping profession, use peer consultation or support groups (like other trainees, colleagues) to debrief tough cases. Knowing others experience similar feelings normalizes it. They might also share coping strategies (like certain boundaries they keep).
  - For personal supporters, find someone you can talk to – ideally without violating the survivor's privacy. Maybe a general support group for caregivers or a private conversation with a therapist about how to manage the stress. Even reading accounts of other caregivers can be validating.
- **Self-Compassion:** Practice what you preach. Treat yourself with the same kindness you'd treat the trauma survivor. Don't guilt-trip yourself for feeling affected ("I shouldn't be tired, it's not even my trauma" – that's unfair to you). Acknowledge that secondary stress is real and valid. Some helpers like to write compassion letters or keep reminders (like, "I'm doing the best I can, and it's okay to take a break when I need it."). Affirm that by caring, you're doing a beautiful thing, but you're human, not an unlimited well.
- **Healthy Boundaries with Work (Literal and Emotional):**

- Therapists: set a time when you stop thinking about work each day. Don't bring case files to bed or constantly check email at midnight. Maybe have a ritual leaving the office – e.g., listen to a favorite upbeat song on the drive home to shift your mindset, or physically say "I am leaving these worries here until tomorrow." Some use a box where they imagine locking the work stuff.
- For personal supporters: when you're having your time (be it at your job or relaxing), try to not be in constant "rescuer mode." It's okay to compartmentalize a bit. It doesn't mean you don't care; it means you care sustainably. If the survivor is safe for the time being, allow yourself to watch that comedy, go out with other friends, etc., without guilt.

- **Self-Care Activities:** Practice what we advised survivors, because it helps helpers too! Ensure you get enough sleep, eat well, exercise (take that walk after an intense session day to burn off adrenaline – it's like shaking off the energy), do relaxing activities (maybe you do your own grounding or mindfulness after hearing a tough story, to recenter yourself). Engage in hobbies or social activities that have nothing to do with trauma. That might feel hard if you see a lot of suffering (you might think "How can I go have fun when people are hurting?"), but remember the suffering won't end sooner because you suffer with them constantly. In fact, you'll be a better helper if you maintain your well-being – you'll have more patience, clarity, and warmth to give.
- **Watch for "Rescue Fantasy":** Many helpers (especially new therapists or loved ones) have a deep desire to make it all better for the survivor. Be mindful if you start over-functioning – like doing things for the person they could do themselves, or getting frustrated if they don't take all your advice. That can lead to burnout and also isn't empowering to them. Check your savior impulses. It's natural to want to fix it (especially if you love them), but remind yourself your role is support, not solve. Keeping that boundary prevents you from feeling so personally responsible for outcomes (which are ultimately out of your control).

- **Vicarious Resilience:** A concept to focus on the positive impact of witnessing someone's healing. Yes, hearing trauma is hard, but seeing someone go from severe pain to coping better, rediscovering hope, etc., can be incredibly uplifting. When you find yourself weighed down, also recall the resilience and courage you see in survivors. Let that inspire you. Many helpers say, "I am changed for the better by witnessing their strength." It's like flipping secondary trauma to "secondary resilience." For every horror story you hear, there's often also a story of perseverance. Hold onto those.
- **Professional Development:** If you're a therapist-in-training, get good training in trauma-specific therapies so you feel equipped (helplessness in the therapist can lead to burnout). Also, consider rotating types of cases if possible so you're not exclusively dealing with the most intense traumas all the time early in your career. If you are drawn to trauma work long-term, maybe engage in advocacy or policy as a macro way to channel any frustration (like working on better mental health resources or prevention programs – turning pain into purpose helps).

- **Personal Therapy or Supervision:** It bears repeating – if you are helping others process trauma, have a space where you can process. Therapists often have their own therapist or at least intermittent therapy for themselves (there's zero shame in that; many find it keeps them balanced). Supervision isn't just about case guidance, but also emotional support – use it. If you're a spouse or friend, consider seeing a counselor just for you, to talk about how your loved one's trauma affects you and learn coping strategies.

Finally, celebrate your role.

It's easy to focus on what's not working or the stress. Take time to acknowledge the good you do: maybe a client said thank you and that your session helped – soak that in; maybe your friend told you they felt better after your talk – appreciate that. Remind yourself why you do this: likely because you care deeply and believe in healing. Keeping that meaning front and center can buffer the tough times.

In summary, to be an effective, compassionate helper, you must also be compassionate to yourself. Boundaries, self-care, and support for you are not luxuries; they're essentials. As flight attendants say, "Put on your own oxygen mask before assisting others." It's not selfish; it ensures you'll be around to assist others for the long haul, and that the assistance will be grounded in stability and empathy, not martyrdom or burnout.

By doing so, you embody a healing presence – showing survivors not only through words but through your calm and balanced demeanor that peace and wholeness are possible. You become a model of resilience in your own right.

As we near the end of our journey through understanding and healing trauma, remember that whether you are a survivor, a supporter, or both, healing is a collective effort.

We heal ourselves, and in doing so, we often help heal those around us – and vice versa. In the concluding section, we'll tie everything together and leave you with a message of hope and empowerment for the road ahead.

FROM TRAUMA TO TRANSFORMATION – HOPE AND GROWTH BEYOND PTSD

Trauma is a chapter of one's life, not the whole story.

We began this book by unraveling the complex ways trauma and PTSD can affect the brain, body, and spirit.

We journeyed through strategies for reclaiming control, from cutting-edge therapies to age-old wisdom in coping.

We confronted the challenges posed by cultural stigma and historical wounds, and we learned how helpers can support survivors without losing themselves.

> *Now, as we conclude, it's time to emphasize the overarching message threading all these chapters together:* ***healing is possible, and not only is it possible, it can lead to profound growth and meaning in one's life.***

If you are a trauma survivor reading this, take a moment to acknowledge how far you've come and the effort you are trying to put into healing – simply by confronting this topic, seeking knowledge, and holding onto hope, you have taken courageous steps.

Healing doesn't mean forgetting what happened or suddenly being exactly who you were before. It means finding a way to weave your trauma into your life's story such that it no longer dictates the narrative – you do.

It means recognizing the strength it took to survive and using that strength to build a new chapter that emphasizes resilience, connection, and purpose.

Many survivors describe a stage where the pain transforms – sometimes into a drive to help others, sometimes into a deeper appreciation for life, often into a clearer sense of priorities.

This phenomenon of **post-traumatic growth (PTG)** is well-documented. It doesn't trivialize the trauma or suggest it was "good" it happened; rather, it shows the human spirit's remarkable ability to extract wisdom and strength from even the darkest experiences.

Not everyone will say "*I'm glad it happened*" – you don't have to. But you might find yourself saying, "*I'm a stronger/more compassionate person because I went through that and healed.*" Or "*I've rebuilt my life in a way that I value more.*"

Think of some of the greatest examples of human resilience: people who survived severe adversity and then became beacons for others – activists, healers, writers, leaders. Their trauma became fuel for change.

Your journey is your own, but you too may find that as you heal, you have a new understanding of yourself and others. You might value relationships more deeply, or discover spiritual insights, or simply realize "*If I can get through that, I can get through anything.*" These are gifts won from the struggle.

Importantly, healing is not a straight line. There may be setbacks – days when symptoms flare up, anniversaries that sting, losses or stresses that evoke old wounds. That's okay. It doesn't mean you've failed or that "PTSD wins."

It means you're human and healing is a **process**. Keep the long view: a bad day or week doesn't erase the overall progress.

Sometimes you may circle back to issues you thought were resolved, at a deeper layer – that's part of the work.

Be patient and gentle with yourself in those moments; use all the tools and support we discussed. Over time, the bad days usually get fewer and farther between, and your confidence in handling them grows.

Eventually, many survivors reach a point where trauma memories no longer hold emotional terror – they become like old photographs: still there, perhaps still sad, but flat, distant, and not intrusive.

No matter how long it's been or how severe the trauma, improvement is possible.

The brain can change (neuroplasticity), the heart can heal, relationships can mend, and new ones can form.

People find love again after violence, they find safety after fear, they find laughter after tears. If you're earlier in the journey and that seems unbelievable right now, hold on to the voices of others who've been there.

Perhaps through support groups or memoirs, read about those further along. They often say they never imagined life could be good again, and yet it became rich and even joyful.

What helps one person may differ from another, but the common thread is perseverance and openness to healing.

To caregivers and therapists, the conclusion is also hopeful: by supporting trauma survivors, you are facilitating not just the reduction of suffering but often the emergence of incredible personal growth.

Secondary trauma is a risk, but secondary inspiration is a reward – seeing someone reclaim their life is deeply fulfilling and confirms why this work matters.

The knowledge and skills you've gained in this book equip you to continue making a difference without losing yourself. And as more of us become trauma-informed – as families, communities, and societies – the easier it will be for survivors to step forward and get help without shame.

The more we spread understanding, the fewer stigmas remain, and the more prevention we can put in place for future potential trauma.

We should also acknowledge that some trauma consequences are chronic; not everyone will eliminate every symptom, and that's okay.

Some survivors manage PTSD or related challenges long-term, similar to a chronic illness. But even then, they often still lead meaningful lives with love, work, creativity, and happiness in the mix. If complete cure isn't attainable, substantial improvement and a life worth living still is. This is where concepts like acceptance (from ACT) play in – you might accept "I have some triggers still, but I know how to handle them, and they don't stop me from living my life."

Before we close, let's revisit the core pillars that have emerged:

- **Knowledge is power:** You've learned what trauma does and that it's not "you going crazy" – it's a human reaction, often with biological underpinnings. With this knowledge, you can externalize the problem ("this is PTSD affecting my brain") and tackle it piece by piece, rather than feeling it's an inherent flaw.
- **You are not alone:** So many people have walked this path. Reach out – connection is the antidote to the isolation trauma brings. Whether it's one friend or a group of peers or an online forum or a therapist, there are others willing to walk alongside you.
- **It's not your fault, but it is your responsibility to heal:** This is a key distinction. You didn't choose the trauma, you didn't ask for these wounds. Blame lies with the event or perpetrator (if applicable), not you. At the same time, the task of healing falls to you (with support). No one else can do that inner work for you. When you fully grasp this, it can be empowering. It means you have control over what happens next – the trauma isn't continuing, you are now in charge of recovery. You have already taken charge by reading this and implementing strategies.
- **Small steps matter:** Healing often happens in micro-steps – the day you step outside for the first time without fear, the night you sleep 4 hours straight when before it was 2, the first time you tell your story to someone and feel heard, the moment you notice you laughed genuinely at a joke. Celebrate these. They are signposts that you're moving forward.
- **Professional help is a strength:** If you haven't already, consider therapy. The therapies we covered (TF-CBT, EMDR, etc.) are there because no one should have to do this alone, and they can accelerate

the process or help in stuck points. If one approach or therapist doesn't fit, try another. Sometimes it takes a couple tries to find the right match – don't give up. You deserve support.

- **Self-Care and Coping Skills are Your Allies:** Keep practicing the breathing, grounding, mindfulness, journaling, or whatever mix works for you. They might seem simple, but they create stability. Over time, they become second nature – new, healthy habits replacing the old hypervigilance and avoidance patterns.
- **Keep Meaning and Purpose in Sight:** Trauma can shake or shatter one's sense of meaning. Part of healing is rebuilding it – maybe in new ways. Think about what gives you meaning. It could be family, creativity, faith, helping others, learning, nature, anything. Engage with those meaning-makers as you heal; they will propel you forward. As Viktor Frankl, a Holocaust survivor and psychiatrist, famously said, "Those who have a 'why' to live can bear with almost any 'how'." Find or remember your "why."
- **Transformation is Possible:** We titled this conclusion "From Trauma to Transformation" because indeed, many survivors don't just go back to baseline; they evolve into someone even wiser or more compassionate. You may find that you become a source of strength for others, an advocate, or simply that you live with a richer appreciation for life's ordinary moments – a sunrise, a good meal, time with loved ones. In that sense, trauma can transform not only the negative (which it certainly does) but, through healing, also transform positive aspects of your life in ways you might never have anticipated. It's not a journey anyone would voluntarily choose, but those who traverse it often emerge with profound insights and empathy.

As we close the pages of this book, we want to leave you with a vision: **Trauma and PTSD are chapters – they have a beginning, and with work, they can have an end**.

The story beyond doesn't erase the scars, but it integrates them as part of a larger narrative of survival, recovery, and growth. You get to author that narrative.

Imagine sometime in the not-too-distant future: you wake up and trauma is not the first thing on your mind. You go about your day, perhaps hardly thinking about it at all. Or if you do think of it, it's without that spike of pain – more like a fact of your life that you know shaped you but no longer controls you.

You're engaged in activities, connected with people, maybe chasing some dream that had been on hold. You realize you're actually living, not just surviving. That state is attainable – many who once felt utterly broken now live fully. Hold that vision and take the steps, one at a time, to get there.

And if you ever doubt yourself, remember what you've overcome already. The worst has happened to you; now the best is what can happen within you. You are brave, you are worthy of healing, and you are capable of it.

Let this conclusion not be an end, but a commencement – the start of a new chapter where trauma is part of your past, and **renewal** is your present and future.

Go forward, step by step, and know that even on the days it feels two steps back, you have a whole community (survivors, helpers, even readers of this book) silently cheering you on.

Your story matters.

Your healing matters.

And the world will be better for your transformation – because a person who has faced darkness and found light becomes a lighthouse for others.

Thank you for allowing this book to accompany you on this journey. We end with a profound respect for your courage and a heartfelt wish for your continued healing and growth.

Healing is not only possible; it is your birthright.

Embrace it, and step into the wholeness that has always been meant for you.

References / Footnotes (for citation context):

The citations in the text correspond to lines from various sources to substantiate facts and statements, demonstrating evidence-based content.

For readability, they were embedded throughout the chapters.

- NIMH: Definition and facts about PTSD.
- Healthline: Neurobiological impact of trauma and therapy effects.
- Mayo Clinic: Symptom clusters of PTSD.
- Verywell Mind: Coping skills for PTSD, including breathing and writing.
- SAMHSA: Principles of trauma-informed care.
- Yale News: Research on intergenerational trauma (epigenetics).

- Psychology Today: Definition of trauma (APA).
- PositivePsychology: Benefits of journaling and acceptance.
- Psychiatry.org: Discussion of stigma across cultures.
- Open Texts & Others: Various trauma treatment descriptions and cultural context.

By synthesizing knowledge and personal insights, 'Understanding and Healing Trauma and PTSD' aims to be a comprehensive guide and a comforting companion on the path from darkness to light.

www.ingramcontent.com/pod-product-compliance
Lightning Source LLC
LaVergne TN
LVHW060041210926
848481LV00013B/3927